Lect

and l   608

Founding Editors:

M. Beckmann
H.P. Künzi

Managing Editors:

Prof. Dr. G. Fandel
Fachbereich Wirtschaftswissenschaften
Fernuniversität Hagen
Feithstr. 140/AVZ II, 58084 Hagen, Germany

Prof. Dr. W. Trockel
Institut für Mathematische Wirtschaftsforschung (IMW)
Universität Bielefeld
Universitätsstr. 25, 33615 Bielefeld, Germany

Editorial Board:

A. Basile, A. Drexl, H. Dawid, K. Inderfurth, W. Kürsten

PierCarlo Nicola

Experimenting with Dynamic Macromodels

Growth and Cycles

Springer

Professor PierCarlo Nicola
Department of Mathematics
University of Milano
Via Saldini 50
20133 Milan
Italy
PierCarlo.Nicola@mat.unimi.it

ISBN 978-3-540-77396-2   e-ISBN 978-3-540-77397-9

DOI 10.1007/978-3-540-77397-9

Lecture Notes in Economics and Mathematical Systems ISSN 0075-8442

Library of Congress Control Number: 2007942558

© 2008 Springer-Verlag Berlin Heidelberg

Production: LE-TEX Jelonek, Schmidt & Vöckler GbR, Leipzig
Cover design: WMX Design GmbH, Heidelberg

Printed on acid-free paper

9 8 7 6 5 4 3 2 1

springer.com

Ai miei cari che ora vivono nell'eternità:
Nonna Valentina, Zia Pina, Mamma, Papà.

Preface

The main aim of this monograph is to demonstrate the power of combining mathematics with numerical experiments, using a computer, to understand the main determinants of the mobilization of a whole economy. To this end, and starting from Solow's 1956 model, we add, in subsequent steps, the labour market, expenditure on research and development (R&D), and public expenditure on infrastructures in order to construct a more flexible model that can be analysed numerically through numerous computer simulations, to show (realistically) how complex time paths can be. We do this by solving the model(s) for the main variables, gross income, labour employment, consumption, etc.

As this is a monograph, no systematic attempt is made to relate the models presented to the literature; the assumption is that the interested reader has some knowledge of published work on macroeconomic growth theory and business cycles. For example, the excellent and complete (as far as completeness can be achieved in a single book) work by Barro and Sala-i-Martin (2004), which contains many references, is a good study of growth theory; and the monograph by Gabisch and Lorenz (1987) is a good example of the work on business cycle models.

Special treatment is reserved for the labour market, since labour is a quite specific input, that differs from all other inputs. Labour may be supplied by families and cannot be produced in the usual material sense, i.e. labour supply is an exogenous variable in every economy.

It is well known that time can be considered either as a continuous or as a discrete variable; in this work time is considered as a discrete variable, since the theoretical discourse seems to flow more easily when decisions are considered in discrete time. Moreover, various time lags that are present in economic activity, e.g. the production lag between inputs and outputs, and those among profits, wages, and their expenditure, are better formalized when time is considered as a discrete variable.

The first paper I published, which introduced the type of research reported here, was in Italian, and its main aim was to examine whether a labour supply curve, taking a reversed S form, could generate endogenous business cycles in the economy. The model was presented in continuous time and, in many instances, it was possible to detect that endogenous cycles were present. In this monograph the model is expressed in discrete time, and is described in Chapter 4. Another English version, in continuous time, first presented at a meeting held in Urbino in September 2004, is Nicola (2005). The extended version of Chapter 5, which includes investment in R&D, is in press, while the model including both R&D and public expenditure, described in Chapter 6, is being presented for the first time.

The chapters that constitute Part 3, represent the bulk of the current monograph, and include numerous computer simulations, implemented by means of MAPLE software. Thus, in a sense, Part 3 of this monograph can be said to belong to that branch of economics known as Computational Economics, described in books by Amman, Kendrick and Rust (eds.) (1996), and Amman, Kendrick and Mercado (eds.) (2006). Although I sometimes provide parameter values that are found in econometric applications, I make no claim to calibrate the parameters concerned, neither do I claim that the results of the simulations in any sense reproduce the dynamic paths of any real economy. My aim is merely to present a set of models capable of reproducing the richness of the trajectories found in real economic data.

The simulations proposed show very clearly that the models presented generate a huge variety of trajectories, from simple stationary states to chaos-like orbits. Moreover, they show how orbits can change qualitatively when some parameters are changed, even by small amounts. In particular, attention is drawn to the reaction coefficient of the wage rate, α, whose aim is to show the reduction, period after period, in the discrepancy between labour supply and demand. Simulations show that its value influences the orbits generated by the various models considered: while for low values of α, e.g. 0.1, trajectories are generally smooth, at high values of α, e.g. 0.5, orbits often become quite irregular, and this fact seems to be of paramount importance to the design of economic policy interventions.

All the models presented are formulated in a "positive economics" environment, meaning that at no time is there recourse to an overall maximization of some objective function. In this monograph, following the cogent proposal of Ramsey (1928), total undiscounted consumption, generated along the whole time horizon, is considered to provide a satisfactory measure of material welfare. By comparing the value of this index in various contexts, i.e. with respect to the simulations implemented here, it is possible to show that the velocity, α, chosen to manipulate the labour market has a strong effect on material welfare: ceteris paribus, increasing the velocity always decreases total consumption, which is at maximum in a stationary state, i.e. when the starting values of the state variables are equal to those corresponding to a stationary state.

In the models presented in this work, no place is given to money. In my opinion, models that include money are not genuine macromodels; they look like extremely reduced micromodels, containing three goods: physical commodity, labour and money. For the same reason I have not considered models containing two material goods: consumption goods and capital goods. Moreover, in order to remain in the specific field of macroeconomic models, I have not considered overlapping generations.

It is useful to conclude this preface with a caveat: while frequently very illuminating, simulations cannot be taken as the last word in the analysis of economic models. Careful manipulation of the parameters, produces a rich mass of seemingly interesting results; however, to interpret the results of these simulations requires a deep understanding of the theoretical aspects of the models. I therefore firmly believe that the last word must always be founded on theory: simulations, although important, should be complementary to such economic analysis.

My warmest thanks go to Giovanni Marseguerra, who read and improved on my manuscript; I am also grateful to the participants in *MDEF 2004* (Urbino, September 2004) for their interesting suggestions. I thank the colleagues who attended my seminar presentation at *Università Cattolica di Milano* in November 2005. Finally, I wish to acknowledge Cynthia Little, for the numerous improvements to my rough English. Responsibility for all remaining errors and opinions is my own.

Milan, January 2008   *PierCarlo Nicola*

Contents

Part I

Basics

1

Foundations of Macroeconomic Dynamics

1.1 Introduction

Economics is a very complex subject of analysis: it involves studying the interactions among a myriad individual agents engaged in the production, exchange, and consumption of a large number of commodities. Mere formal description, by means of a mathematical model, of a particular economy at a single point of time, or in a single time period, first proposed by Leon Walras (1874–77), is far from straightforward. However, the "setting in motion" of such a model is generally extremely demanding, and sometimes requires some drastic simplifications. Therefore, theoretical economists invented macroeconomic models, a branch of economic theory which, by aggregating all commodities in a very limited number, usually two, one commodity and the labour, can be applied to analyse the main dynamic properties of an economy, such as growth and cycles. These somewhat elementary observations are intended as justification for this monograph.

The first author to provide major stimulus to the formulation and analysis of macroeconomic models is undoubtedly Keynes (1936), but, of course, macroeconomic models were known to economists well before 1936. This monograph does not aim to present a summary of macroeconomic models since their introduction: rather, we start from the well known dynamic model presented by Solow in 1956.

Before presenting the model, it is interesting to look at the very interesting link that exists between macromodels and the standard Walrasian model of general competitive equilibrium. Assume there are two consumable goods, leisure (B) and consumption (C). Given the technologies familiar to firms and the total resources at the disposal of the same set of firms, suppose there is a smooth downward-sloping efficiency frontier in the production of the two goods, depicted by curve P–P in Figure 1.1. Also referring to Figure 1.1, assume that consumers have a common or an average utility function, one of whose indifference curves is given by U–U, which is at a tangent to curve P–P at point E. It is well known that, due to the strict convexity of curve U–U, and

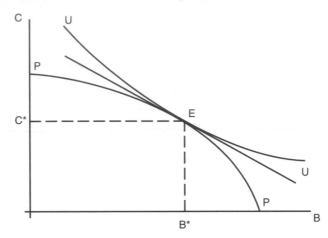

Fig. 1.1. General Equilibrium

the strict concavity of curve P–P, as depicted in Figure 1.1, the slope of the tangent at E common to both curves equals the negative of the equilibrium price ratio[1] of the two goods, this ratio being the general equilibrium price ratio, w/p, where w means the wage rate and p the price of the consumption good, while B^* and C^* are the equilibrium amounts, respectively, of leisure and consumption. Of course, in this interpretation Figure 1.1 can only show the consumption sphere of the economy, while the production sphere remains in the background, except for its efficiency frontier.

1.2 Growth and Cycles

The principal aim of mankind seems to be happiness, but this goal is so far away that economics per se has only a limited number of tools able to promote felicity. In addition, material welfare, measured by per capita GDP (gross domestic product),[2] in general, is positively correlated with the living standards of individuals in an economy, hence with happiness. It is obvious, e.g., that populations in sub Saharan Africa generally live in worse conditions than Western European populations. Therefore, in terms of economic conditions, per capita GDP can be considered a relevant index of the performance of an economy. This means that, in every real economy, collecting data on GDP, year on year, is an important economic statistics task. As an index of the performance of an economy, with respect to that of other

---

[1] I.e., the price ratio at which the quantities of each commodity demanded and supplied are equal.
[2] Despite GDP sometimes being questioned as a relevant measure of economic performance.

economies, the *rate of growth* of GDP[3] is very important. For a generic year t, this index is measured by $(GDP_t - GDP_{t-1})/GDP_{t-1}$; comparing the rates of growth of various countries for a number of years allows applied and theoretical economists, to assess how these countries perform along a given time horizon.[4]

To get an idea of the importance of the rate of growth of an economy for the dimension of GDP, let us take a century as the time interval, and assume that, on average, a hypothetical economy will experience one of the annual rates of growth (r) in the first column of Table 1; normalizing GDP to a starting value of 1, the second column (Y) gives the value of GDP at the end of the century, based on the rates in the first column:

r	Y
0.005	1.647
0.01	2.705
0.015	4.432
0.02	7.245
0.03	19
0.05	131
0.07	867
0.09	5,529
0.10	13,780

The formula employed to obtain Y numbers is compound interest, i.e. $Y = (1+r)^n$, where r is the annual rate of growth, and n, here equal to 100, is the number of years considered.

In terms of some world economies, an annual rate of 1% is an average rate for the European Union countries for the early years of the XXI century: according to Table 1, then, these economies would grow less than threefold in a century. If one considers a country such as the UK, presently growing at about 3% annually, its economic dimension after a century could be 19 times its starting dimension, a very respectable dimension compared to a 1% growth rate. If we consider the present annual rate of growth of China, equal to at least 9%, the result would be an astonishing 5,529 times the starting value, which seems totally impossible as the average for a century, given the extremely wide dimension based on China's actual population, and given the limited disposability of land (and of sea) on the earth. For the world economy, it would seem that an average annual rate around 3%, and a 19 fold increase in GDP over a century, are more or less the highest rates possible.

---

[3] To account for the dimension of an economy, as measured by its population, the rate of growth of per capita GDP is of course a more indicative index.

[4] See Barro and Sala-i-Martin (2004, Chapter 1) for a good presentation and discussion on rates of growth for almost all countries in the world.

We now turn briefly to some arithmetics of growth. Assume that the quantity Y grows in time at the rate r_t in period t; thus we have $Y_t = (1+r_t)Y_{t-1}$, for $t = 1, 2, \ldots$, where Y_t denotes the value at the end of period t, running from $t - 1$ to t. At the end of a time horizon of n periods the average rate of growth, r, is the number verifying

$$\prod_{t=1}^{n}(1 + r_t) = (1 + r)^n,$$

i.e.

$$r = \left[\prod_{t=1}^{n}(1 + r_t)\right]^{1/n} - 1.$$

On the basis of the preceding formula, $Y_t = (1 + r_t)Y_{t-1}$, the last formula becomes

$$r = (Y_n/Y_0)^{1/n} - 1,$$

i.e. the average rate of growth, r, can be calculated directly once we know the starting and the last values of the variable under consideration. In many comparisons for the computer generated experimental results implemented in Part 3 of this monograph, the value taken by r will summarize the dynamics of the simulated economy.

Real world economies, and some third world economies, generally grow, year on year, at a positive and variable rate. This means that there are economic cycles that move around an increasing trend. Of course, cycles are not one of the primary aims of an economy, but generally are unavoidable, having multiple causes from real, to monetary, to psychological.[5] When we come to the computer simulations, presented in Part 3, it will be possible to realize, by means of the results summarized in Chapter 13, that, ceteris paribus, cycles generally cause an economy to enjoy a total consumption level, extended to the whole time horizon, which is significantly less than the total consumption that would have been possible were cycles absent, or occurring at very long periodicity.

1.3 Solow's Model: Continuous Time Version

In a sense, Solow (1956) can be said to be the founding model of dynamic macroeconomics. However, it should be noted that in the same year Swan (1956) published a very similar model. Before presenting the mathematical apparatus formalizing this model, it is useful to illustrate it (see Figure 1.2). The horizontal axis, labelled k, measures per capita capital, i.e. the amount of capital per unit of labour; curve $sf(k)$ denotes the per capita production function, or the output per unit of labour, $f(k)$, which is assumed to manifest

---

[5] See, e.g., the models studied by Gabisch and Lorenz (1987).

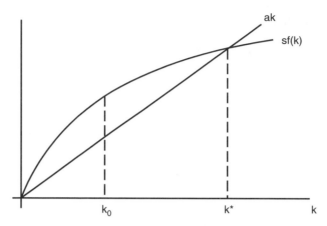

Fig. 1.2. Solow's Endogenous Growth

decreasing returns to scale, multiplied by the savings rate, s. Thus, $sf(k)$ measures gross investment, which is a positive force acting on the growth of the economy. The straight line, labelled ak, represents negative forces, i.e. the capital depreciation rate plus the labour force growth rate, contrasting with the growth in per capita capital. The quantity k^* is the positive stationary value of per capita capital, i.e. the value at which per capita capital does not change over time. If the starting value of per capita capital is k_0 then, as both Figure 1.2 and the analysis below show, $k(t)$ increases monotonically, in real time, to the stationary value k^*. On the other hand, if $k_0 > k^*$, per capita capital would be decreasing over time to k^*.

If we formally consider time, denoted by t, as a continuous variable, with $t = 0$ as the conventionally chosen starting time, the variables in Solow's model, interpreted as intensities, are:

$N(t)$ the (fully) employed labour supply at time t;
$K(t)$ the amount of capital going into production at time t;
$Y(t)$ gross output, or GDP, at time t;
$C(t)$ consumption at time t.

The mathematical formulae linking the above variables are:

$$Y(t) = F[K(t), N(t)] \tag{3.1}$$

i.e.: F denoting the production function, verifying

$$F(0, N) = 0 = F(K, 0),$$

maximum output at time t is a function of the quantities of inputs into production.

$$\dot{N}(t) = \nu N(t), \tag{3.2}$$

i.e., the rate of change in the labour force (and in the population), $\dot{N}(t) = \frac{dN(t)}{dt}$, is proportional, according to intensity ν, to the existing labour force. If $N_0 > 0$ means population at the starting time, then this equation is easily solved to give the exponential function

$$N(t) = N_0 \exp(\nu t). \tag{3.3}$$

In the simplest case, and according to Keynes, consumption is a given fraction of income,[6] i.e.:

$$C(t) = \gamma Y(t) \qquad (0 < \gamma < 1); \tag{3.4}$$

γ is the well known propensity to consume.

Assuming that the instantaneous rate of depreciation of capital is δ, verifying $0 \leq \delta \leq 1$, the rate of change in capital is

$$\dot{K}(t) = F[K(t), N(t)] - \delta K(t) - C(t), \tag{3.5}$$

or total gross output, minus capital depreciation, minus consumption (which is the part of output subtracted from production) and expresses net investment, which is added to capital (if positive), or subtracted from capital (if negative).

As customary, let us assume that F is positively homogeneous at degree 1,[7] or $F(\alpha K, \alpha N) = \alpha F(K, N)$, for all non negative values of K, N, α. Then, choosing $\alpha = 1/N$ ($N > 0$), this equality can be written as

$$F(K/N, N/N) = 1/N F(K, N).$$

Thus, based on (3.4), we can write (3.5) as follows:

$$\dot{K}(t) = (1 - \gamma)N(t)F[K(t)/N(t), 1] - \delta K(t). \tag{3.6}$$

We now introduce another variable, $k = K/N$, denoting per capita capital, and can write $s = 1 - \gamma$, which is the savings rate; moreover, we can write $f(k) = F(K/N, 1)$, implying $f(0) = 0$, and thus calculate $\dot{k}(t) = d[K(t)/N(t)]/dt = \dot{K}(t)/N(t) - \nu K(t)/N(t)$. Then we can write equation (3.6) as:

$$\dot{k} = sf(k) - (\delta + \nu)k, \tag{3.7}$$

where, for reasons of simplification, the time notation is suppressed. Equation (3.7) is an autonomous differential equation in the only variable k, and is easily solved qualitatively by graphically drawing the two terms forming the right hand side of (3.7). Writing $a = \delta + \nu > 0$, we obtain Figure 1.2 above. From this

---

[6] This assumption is one of the main drawbacks of the Solow–Swan model.
[7] I.e., returns to scale are constant.

figure it is apparent that there are two stationary solutions to (3.7), i.e. $k = 0$ and $k = k^*$, where k^* is the positive value satisfying $sf(k) - (\delta + \nu)k = 0$, or

$$k^* = \frac{s}{\delta + \nu} f(k^*).$$

The first, uninteresting from an economic viewpoint, solution is a repeller of the trajectories solving (3.7), k^* is an attractor, so that starting from any $k_0 > 0$ we have $\lim_{t \to \infty} k(t) = k^*$. Once this value has been reached, both total capital, $K(t)$, and labour, $N(t)$, grow at the same rate, ν, which also becomes the growth rate of income and of consumption. Thus, it can be said that, when k_0 is smaller then k^* the economy is a relatively poor one, and must make efforts to accumulate capital at a rate that is greater than the exogenous rate of population growth, while for $k_0 > k^*$ the reverse is true.

It is clear that the determinants of growth in this model economy are twofold: accumulation of capital, i.e. net investment and population growth. Of course, in real world economies other factors, such as technical progress, are responsible for economic growth, as we will show later. Here we focus on the fact that the savings rate, s, is exogenously given, i.e. $s = 1 - \gamma$; when, if ever, the steady state value is reached, k^*, all per capita variables become stationary. In particular, per capita consumption is

$$c^* = (1 - s)f(k^*) = f(k^*) - sf(k^*) = f(k^*) - (\nu + \delta)k^*.$$

All else being given, Figure 1.2 shows that k^* is an increasing function of s; it is useful to denote this dependence by writing $k^*(s)$, and also $c^*(s)$. For $s = 0$ nothing is saved and we have $k^*(0) = 0$, and thus $c^*(0) = 0$; for $s = 1$ everything is saved and we have $c^*(1) = 0$. Since $c^*(s)$ is a continuous function of s, in the interval $[0, 1]$ there is a value of s maximizing per–capita consumption. According to the previous relation on c^*, this maximizing value is the solution to the equation $f'[k^*(s)] - (\nu + \delta) = 0$. Given the assumption $f''(k) < 0$ everywhere, this equation has only one maximizing solution, s^*, meaning that if the saving rate equals this value then, in a steady state, per capita consumption is maximized, its value being $c^*(s^*)$. Suppose that we have $k_0 = k^*(s^*)$, all persons living at all times will enjoy the same (maximum) per capita consumption: there is no advantage for the present generation over all future generations. This particular ideal state of the economy has been termed by Phelps *golden rule of capital accumulation*. In the models implemented in Part 3 the savings rate is not given, but is determined endogenously; thus the golden rule has no sensible role to play in these models.

1.4 Harrod–Domar's Alternative

It is of some historical interest to consider the preceding model when there is no production function, F, exhibiting an infinite range of possible technical coefficients, but where capital and labour can be efficiently combined only in fixed proportions, according to a Leontief production function.[8]

Instead of the production function, F, we assume that capital and labour generate output according to the following function:

$$(K, N) \mapsto F^*(K, N) = \min\{a_k K, a_n N\}, \tag{4.1}$$

where a_k, a_n are positive coefficients. Now instead of (3.1) we have relation

$$Y(t) = \min\{a_k K(t), a_n N(t)\}, \tag{4.2}$$

while relations (3.2)–(3.5) still hold true.

This model introduces the "knife-edge" problem, i.e. the highly probable case that either capital or labour are partly unemployed. Indeed, let us assume that at time $t = 0$ we have $a_k K(0) = a_n N(0)$; then we have $Y(0) = a_k K(0) = a_n N(0)$, and by substitution in (3.6) we obtain

$$\dot{K}(0) = [sa_k - \delta]K(0). \tag{4.3}$$

Since labour grows at rate ν, in order to keep full employment of both labour and capital, for all ts, capital must also grow at the same rate ν; then, according to (4.3), the following relation will hold true:

$$sa_k - \delta = \nu. \tag{4.4}$$

But, since the values taken by all these quantities are exogenous to the model, it is only by chance that the aptly named "knife-edge" relation (4.4) is verified. In general, there will be underemployment either of labour or of capital.

We should not forget that there is a third possibility; there is also a linear programming production model, which assumes that there is a finite set of constant returns to scale efficient techniques; of course, this model lies between the Solow and Harrod-Domar models. Indeed, if there are m distinct production processes, $(a_k^j, a_n^j)(j = 1, 2, \ldots, m)$, then full employment of both capital and labour occurs when the capital coefficient of the model takes one of these possible m values, say a_k^*, and this value satisfies relation (4.4). Thus, the existence of many techniques increases the probability of full employment for both factors.

1.5 Discrete Time Formulation of Solow's Model

Let us now assume that time is expressed by an integer variable, $t = 0, 1, 2, 3, \ldots$, and the time horizon forms a sequence of periods, whose lengths are conventionally chosen equal to 1. Considering time this way, the variables

---

[8] Described in Chapter 3.

are no longer intensities, but become effective quantities. The absolute rate of change of capital is no longer expressed by the time derivative, $\dot{K}$, but is measured by the first difference, $\Delta K_t = K_{t+1} - K_t$, while the equation governing population dynamics is written as $N_t = N_0(1 + \nu)^t$. Assuming that period t runs from dates $t - 1$ and t, and considering all variables refer to the start of each period, we can say that production takes exactly one time period to materialize, i.e. that inputs applied at the start of a period give the corresponding output only at the end of the same period, which is also the start of the next period.

The discrete time equations in Solow's model, which is presented and discussed in Section 3 when time is continuous, bearing in mind that $F(K, N)$ denotes gross output, are as follows:

$$Y_{t+1} = F(K_t, N_t),$$

$$N_t = N_0(1 + \nu)^t \qquad (\nu > 0),$$

$$C_t = \gamma Y_t \qquad (0 < \gamma < 1),$$

$$K_{t+1} + C_{t+1} = Y_{t+1} + (1 - \delta)K_t \qquad (0 \le \delta \le 1).$$

Inserting the first and third relations into the last, and remembering that $s = 1 - \gamma$, we have:

$$K_{t+1} = sF(K_t, N_t) + (1 - \delta)K_t. \tag{5.1}$$

Since the production function, F, has been assumed to be homogeneous at degree one, introducing per capita capital, $k_t = K_t/N_t$, we have $k_{t+1} = K_{t+1}/N_{t+1} = K_{t+1}/N_t \cdot N_t/N_{t+1} = K_{t+1}/N_t \cdot [1/(1+\nu)]$, and equation (5.1), dividing both sides by N_t, reads:

$$k_{t+1} = \frac{s}{1+\nu}f(k_t) + \frac{1-\delta}{1+\nu}k_t. \tag{5.2}$$

If we write this equation as follows:

$$\Delta k_t = \frac{s}{1+\nu}f(k_t) - \frac{\nu+\delta}{1+\nu}k_t,$$

considering $\frac{s}{1+\nu}$ instead of s, putting $a = \frac{\nu+\delta}{1+\nu}$, and with Δk_t on the vertical axis, Figure 1.2 holds as an illustration of equation (5.2) and its solution. In particular, provided that $\nu + \delta > 0$, the positive stationary solution of (5.2),

$$k^* = \frac{s}{\nu+\delta}f(k^*),$$

determines the value described in the continuous version of the model; clearly, k^* is the attractor for all solutions to the difference equation (5.2).

1.6 Continuous Versus Discrete Time

Both calendar and psychological time seem to flow continuously. But human decisions appear to be made and implemented only from time to time. Hence, here it seems economically more meaningful to present our models in discrete time. It is plain that a model expressed in continuous time can be reformulated in discrete time, and vice versa. What is important to remember is that in discrete time a variable, e.g. $x(t)$, expresses the value it takes in a specified time period, t, while in continuous time $x(t)$ denotes the instantaneous intensity of the phenomenon being considered: i.e., it is $x(t)\Delta t$ that measures the effective quantity associated with a small time interval $\Delta t > 0$.

To show quickly and very simply how to translate a model from continuous to discrete time, and vice versa, we assume that in continuous time $x(t)$ obeys the differential equation $\dot{x}(t) = f[x(t)]$, where $\dot{x}(t)$ means $dx(t)/dt$. Now, bearing in mind the meaning of the time derivative, $\frac{dx(t)}{dt} \approx \frac{x(t+\Delta t)-x(t)}{\Delta t}$, for small values of Δt, the previous differential equation can be written as:

$$\frac{x(t + \Delta t) - x(t)}{\Delta t} = f[x(t)],$$

or

$$x(t + \Delta t) = x(t) + \Delta t f[x(t)], \tag{6.1}$$

which, of course, becomes the preceding differential equation for $\Delta t \to 0$.

Let us now assume that it is acceptable to take $\Delta t = 1$;[9] then (6.1) becomes $x(t + 1) = x(t) + f[x(t)] = \Phi[x(t)]$, which is a first order difference equation approximating the differential equation $\dot{x}(t) = f[x(t)]$.

From here on, we will write $x(t)$ to denote the intensity of a variable at time t, and x_t to denote a quantity referred to **period** t, meaning the time interval $[t - 1, t]$.

1.7 Aggregation

Every economy encompasses a large number of commodities; thus the quantities of commodities, and their prices, must be represented by vectors. How is it possible to translate a vector of the quantities of the various goods into a scalar? We suppose there are n goods, whose quantities are expressed by means of a non negative n-vector, $x = (x_1, x_2, \ldots, x_n)$, and assume that the given is a positive price n-vector, $p = (p_1, p_2, \ldots, p_n)$. Taking the inner product of these two vectors, we obtain the aggregate macro variable X, i.e.

$$X = p \cdot x = \sum_i p_i x_i, \tag{7.1}$$

---

[9] Of course, a unit time interval physically has no precise meaning; the unit of time can be chosen to be very short.

which depends on the choice of p and, at the aggregate macroeconomic level, summarizes the vector of quantities x.[10] Of course, the loss of information in passing from vector x to scalar X is substantial, but in macroeconomics it is assumed that such loss is acceptable, since the main interest, in general, is to study the determinants of the time evolution of the major economic aggregates. These simple considerations must be kept in mind when interpreting the models presented in this monograph.

---

[10] E.g., with reference to Solow's model, consumption, C, is the value of all goods consumed; income, Y, is the value of all goods produced, etc., etc.

2

Population Dynamics and the Labour Market

2.1 Laws of Population Dynamics

2.1.1 Continuous Time Laws

Of all production factors, labour is certainly the most important and specific; it is deserving of very deep consideration and there have been numerous articles and books published on this subject. A very extensive collection of papers on labour is contained in the five volumes titled *Handbook of Labour Economics* (1986–), edited by Ashenfelter et al. Of course, labour is supplied by people, and thus, ceteris paribus, is a function of the number of people in the economy. Hence, it is important to consider the laws governing population dynamics. We consider two alternative laws for the time evolution of a population: steady growth law and logistic growth law. In continuous time, we can write $P(t)$ for population at time t; **steady growth law** is obtained when, given a generally positive instantaneous rate of growth, ν, the differential equation for population dynamics is:

$$\dot{P}(t) = dP(t)/dt = \nu P(t). \tag{1.1}$$

Given the starting population, $P(0) > 0$, the solution to this equation is

$$P(t) = P(0) \exp(\nu t).$$

This is the function employed in Chapter 1, to present Solow's model. When ν is positive, equation (1.1) says that population increases steadily, with no upper bound; of course, this type of time behaviour is completely unrealistic in the very long run.

The other main differential equation governing population growth is the so-called **logistic law**, introduced by the Belgian mathematician Verhulst in the 19th century. Given two positive parameters, ζ and ξ, this law can be written as:

$$\dot{P}(t) = \zeta P(t) - \xi [P(t)]^2. \tag{1.2}$$

In this equation, the quadratic term acts as a negative force, e.g. due to the overcrowding of a given territory when population exceeds some "carrying capacity", which is opposed to the positive force expressed by the first term. Integrating (1.2) by parts, given a positive starting value, $P(0)$, verifying $\zeta - \xi P(0) > 0$, and defining $H = \frac{P(0)}{\zeta - \xi P(0)}$, the solution to this equation is

$$P(t) = \frac{\zeta H}{\xi H + \exp(-\zeta t)}.$$

Assume that $P(0)$ has a value such that $\dot{P}(t)$ is positive for $t = 0$. From the previous formula it is clear that when $t \to -\infty$ then $P(t)$ goes to zero, through positive values, while for $t \to \infty$ population asymptotically takes the value $P^* = \zeta/\xi$; thus, the value of $P(t)$ is upper bounded. This means that for values of $P(0)$ satisfying $0 < P(0) < P^*$, the right hand side of equation (1.2) being positive, population increases, while for values of $P(0)$ such that $P(0) > P^*$, the right hand side of (1.2) is negative and population decreases in time, from $P(0)$ to P^*. The next figure, drawn for $P(0) < P^*$, depicts the time behaviour of $P(t)$:

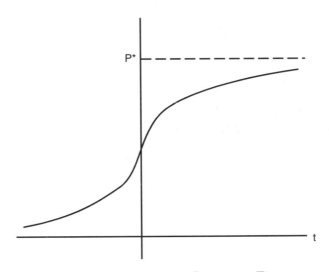

Fig. 2.1. Logistic Law in Continuous Time

While this law of population dynamics is more realistic than steady growth law, experimentally it has been shown that the value taken by ζ/ξ may change over time, so that in the very long run the logistic law does not simulate in a completely satisfactory way how human populations evolve over time.

2.1.2 Discrete Time Laws

Considering time as a discrete variable, $t = 0, 1, 2, 3, \ldots$, steady growth law is expressed by the equation

$$P_{t+1} = (1 + \nu)P_t, \tag{1.3}$$

which replaces (1.1). Its solution, given $P_0 > 0$, is

$$P_t = P_0(1 + \nu)^t \qquad (t = 0, 1, 2, 3, \ldots);$$

if ν is positive, this function states that population increases over time constantly at the rate ν.

The discrete time equivalent of the logistic law (1.2) is

$$P_{t+1} = \zeta P_t - \xi P_t^2. \tag{1.4}$$

Contrary to what is true for its continuous time equivalent, somewhat surprisingly, the solution to this equation, except for particular values of the parameters cannot be expressed by a finite number of symbols;[1] but, of course, through iteration any sequence $\{P_t\}_0^\infty$, can be generated for every given P_0. For this reason, it is better to introduce a change of variable, allowing us to write (1.4) as an equation with only one parameter. To this end, let us put $Q_t = (\xi/\zeta)P_t$, and write (1.4) as follows: $(\xi/\zeta)P_{t+1} = \zeta(\xi/\zeta)P_t[1 - (\xi/\zeta)P_t]$; then equation (1.4) becomes

$$Q_{t+1} = \zeta Q_t(1 - Q_t). \tag{1.5}$$

Since P_t must always be non negative, from equation (1.5) it appears that Q_t must belong to the unit interval I, $I = [0, 1]$, and that ζ must take values in the interval $(0, 4]$, to have $Q_t \in I$ for every $t = 0, 1, 2, 3, \ldots$.

Equation (1.5) is known, in modern dynamic systems theory, as a **quadratic map**, and it is well known that its trajectories may be very complex, and even chaotic in the proper sense of this term within chaos theory, when the parameter ζ approaches the value 4. In contrast, the solution to the corresponding differential equation has a simple reversed S shaped form, the same for all parameter values, as shown in Figure 2.1. Despite the fact that in general one cannot write a formula for the solution to equation (1.5), it is clear that by iteration one can generate any orbit for every possible starting value Q_0.

Since the logistic law can generate time paths that are qualitatively extremely different from one another according to the values assigned to the parameters, let us consider the time evolution of the population for two different choices of parameter values, but the same starting value in both cases, i.e. $P_0 = 100$. The first time path corresponds to parameters $\zeta = 2.5$ and

---

[1] See, e.g., Agarwal (1992, pp. 119–121).

$\xi = 0.0125$. The time evolution of population, $\{P_t\}$ (plotted in Figure 11.1 in Chapter 11), shows that the corresponding positive stationary value is $P^* = 120$. It is plain that there are strongly decreasing oscillations in the first ten periods, after which population reaches its stationary value.

The second time evolution of P_t (depicted in Figure 11.2 in Chapter 11 for $t = 0, 1, 2, \ldots, 120$), is generated by $P_0 = 100$ and the following parameter values: $\zeta = 4$, $\xi = 0.008$, for which there is a corresponding positive stationary value $P^* = 375$. It can be seen that there is a chaotic-like time path: oscillations are irregular and there is no dumping over time. The population dimension continuously oscillates between a very small positive value, approximately 0.0105, and its extreme value of 500. A similar result is obtained with an even longer time horizon, e.g. 1,200 time periods.

Of course, this very complex time behaviour of the logistic equation is well known in deterministic chaos theory. Although chaotic trajectories may appear very interesting in many applied sciences, it is difficult to believe that a population is subjected to such wide changes, from period to period. Thus, in the simulations in Part 3, parameters are chosen such that population experiences only mild variations from period to period.

2.2 Labour Supply

The greatest proportion of the existing work on macroeconomic models, such as the Solow–Swan model described in Chapter 1, Section 3, that are not specifically devoted to studying the labour market, see labour as permanently fully employed. Hence, they see no need to distinguish between demand and supply. Because the labour market is probably the most important of all specific markets, as labour is essential to the production of every commodity and is also the primary source of family incomes, in this monograph we propose and analyse a labour market, whose two sides we consider separately and whose interaction we examine. This separation seems a useful approach to economic policy problem analysis.[2]

Assuming labour supply to be a function of real wage rates, w/p, for sufficiently high wage rates this supply decreases for a while, as a result of the income effect overcoming the substitution effect (giving to labour supply the characteristic of a 'Giffen commodity' placed on the supply side of the economy), then increases again to a maximum amount, measuring total supply by the existing labour force, usually a given fraction of the existing population. This makes it possible to generate endogenous business cycles, as we will see in Part 3.[3]

---

[2] A detailed analysis of the labour market, with many implications for economic policy, is proposed by Solow (1994).

[3] E.g., a backward bending labour supply curve as discussed in Samuelson (1970, pp. 553–554). See also the Appendix, where a reversed S shaped market supply curve is shown to be derived by aggregating individual labour supply functions.

The form of the supply function we consider here can be expressed by a cubic function,

$$L = \min\left\{\bar{L}, \max\{0, -a_0 + a_1 w/p - a_2(w/p)^2 + a_3(w/p)^3\}\right\}; \qquad (2.1)$$

when all parameters are positive, its graph looks as in Figure 2.2.

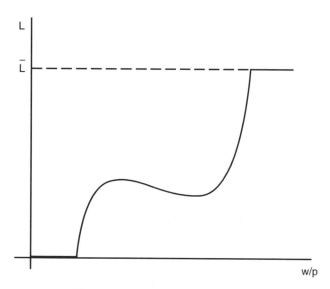

Fig. 2.2. Labour Supply Function

The first horizontal tract of the curve means that if the real wage rate is less than a (vital) minimum, i.e. the real and positive solution to equation $-a_0 + a_1 w/p - a_2(w/p)^2 + a_3(w/p)^3 = 0$, labour supply is zero; the last horizontal tract means that, in the case that population is stationary, the supply of labour is upper bounded by the physiological maximum quantity $\bar{L}$.

More interestingly, we could assume that $\bar{L}$ is moving in time; the dynamics of the population then would follow either the exponential growth law (1.3), or the logistic law (1.4). In either case the upper bound in (2.1), i.e. $\bar{L}$, moves with time, and the labour supply function changes, but in line with the form shown in Figure 2.2. The case being as stated, and assuming that the labour force is a fixed percentage, $v, 0 < v < 1$, of total population, in (2.1) in place of $\bar{L}$ we have the quantity $vP(t)$; thus (2.1) becomes:

$$L(t) = \min\left\{vP(t), \max\{0, -a_0 + a_1 w/p - a_2(w/p)^2 + a_3(w/p)^3\}\right\}. \qquad (2.2)$$

In the computer simulations implemented in Part 3, experiments are presented according to these various labour supply functions.

2.3 Labour Demand

Labour demand comes from the set of firms active in the economy. In this monograph it is assumed that production occurs under competitive conditions, so that an equilibrium condition for the set of firms is: labour productivity equals real wage rate, w/p. In formulae, let us consider an aggregate production function, $F : \Re_+^2 \to \Re_+$, by means of which $F(K, X)$ denotes maximum output obtained by the quantities K of capital, and X of labour. If we assume that F is differentiable, and at least of class C^2, and write $\frac{\partial F(K,X)}{\partial X} = F_X(K, X)$, then a necessary condition to be verified by the optimal amount of labour demanded is:

$$F_X(K, X) - w/p = 0. \tag{3.1}$$

Assuming that both marginal productivities of F are positive and, moreover, that $\frac{\partial^2 F}{\partial X^2} = F_{XX} < 0$ always, we can invert the previous equality, substituting N for X to mean the optimal quantity of labour chosen by firms, to obtain

$$N = F_X^{-1}(w/p; K). \tag{3.2}$$

Moreover, given $K > 0$, we can assume that $\lim_{X \to 0+} F_X(K, X) = +\infty$, and $\lim_{X \to \infty} F_X(K, X) = 0^+$, known as Inada's conditions; this implies that F_X^{-1} takes all values between $+\infty$ and 0. So the graph of function (3.2), for given $K > 0$, looks as in Figure 2.3.

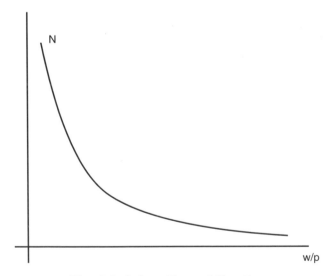

Fig. 2.3. Labour Demand Function

2.4 Market Equilibrium

Function (2.1) expresses labour supply, while for a given positive value of K, (3.2) is the labour demand function. The labour market is in (temporary) equilibrium when firms' employment equals the minimum of these two quantities. If we use E to denote the effective quantity of labour employed by the production sector, its value is expressed by

$$E = \min\{L, N\}. \tag{4.1}$$

In this monograph, equilibrium employment will be considered as measured by the quantity E. Clearly, when N does not equal L some rationing must occur in the labour market: for $N < L$ workers are partly rationed, while $L < N$ means firms are rationed.[4] Of course, given $K > 0$, there is always a real wage rate clearing the labour market. In general, the equilibrium values of w/p can be 1, or 2, or 3, as shown in Figure 2.4. Note that the case where there are exactly two equilibrium real wage rates is not generic, because labour demand and supply curves must meet in a specific way. In particular, Figure 2.4 depicts the case where there are three possible equilibrium wages for w/p; it is clear that, by considering w/p variable in time according to the difference $N - L$,[5] the first and third solutions are stable, while the second is unstable. This is one of the causes of a business cycle in the macroeconomic models presented in Part 3.

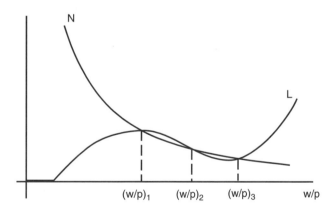

Fig. 2.4. Labour Market Equilibrium

---

[4] In this monograph no attempt is made to study how potential workers are matched to firms; but there are numerous papers devoted to the study of matching processes, starting from Phelps (1968) contribution; see, e.g., Wapler (2003, Ch.3), and his references.

[5] See Chapter 4, equation (2.10), and the accompanying discussion.

3

Production Functions

3.1 Introduction

There are numerous production functions that can be used in applied macro-economic models. Here we consider the three most common ones: Cobb–Douglas, Constant Elasticity of Substitution (CES), and fixed coefficients, or Leontief, functions.[1] We should mention also the so called returns to scale. The simplest case to consider in the analysis of macro models, for all types of production functions, is constant returns to scale, i.e. multiplying all inputs by a positive constant, thus keeping the ratios among all inputs unchanged, results in an output multiplied by the same constant. If $z = (z_1, z_2, \ldots, z_n) \in \Re^n_+$ denotes a vector of n inputs and $f : \Re^n_+ \to \Re_+$ is the production function for maximum output, y, obtained from a given z, or $y = f(z)$, then f is positively homogeneous to degree r, a positive number, when for every $\alpha > 0$, and every z, one has

$$f(\alpha z) = \alpha^r f(z).$$

In economics a very important and meaningful result on differentiable homogeneous functions is expressed by the following property, first proved by the Swiss mathematician, Euler:

$$r f(z) = \sum_{i=1}^{n} z_i \partial f(z)/\partial z_i.$$

The economic importance of this property is that, in the firm problem under competitive conditions, a first order condition to obtain maximum profit, when all factors are employed in positive quantities, is that the marginal value of every input, $p \partial f(z)/\partial z_i$ $(i = 1, 2, \ldots, n)$, p being the output price, equals the corresponding input price, p_i, or:

$$p \partial f(z) \partial z_i = p_i \qquad\qquad (i = 1, 2, \ldots, n).$$

---

[1] Although in this monograph all production functions considered contain only two types of inputs, labour and capital, in this chapter the production functions are written as depending on n distinct inputs.

Inserting these equalities into Euler's formula yields $rpf(z) = \sum_i p_i z_i$, thus

$$(1 - r)pf(z)$$

measures firm's profit, which is positive for $r < 1$, i.e. when there are decreasing returns to scale, zero for $r = 1$, and negative for $r > 1$, i.e. when returns to scale are increasing. This result explains the frequent statement that "increasing returns to scale and perfect competition are incompatible".

In the models presented in Part 2, we always assume that the production function is positively homogeneous at degree 1.

3.2 Cobb–Douglas Production Functions

The general production function, with n inputs, proposed by Cobb and Douglas, is written

$$z \mapsto f(z) = a \prod_{i=1}^{n} z_i^{\alpha_i}, \tag{2.1}$$

where a and α_is are positive constants. Equation (2.1) implies that $f(z) > 0$ if and only if all elements of z are positive. It is plain that (2.1) is positively homogeneous at degree $r = \sum_i \alpha_i$. Its level curves, corresponding to a given positive output, $\bar{y}$, are branches of hyperbolae, with the coordinate axes as asymptotes. For $n = 2$, a level curve looks as follows:

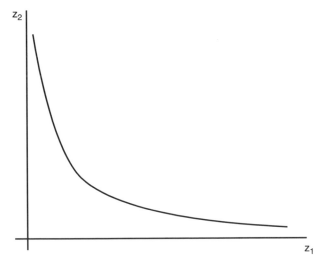

Fig. 3.1. A Cobb–Douglas' Level Curve

The marginal productivities of function (2.1) are:

$$f_i(z) = \frac{\partial f}{\partial z_i}(z) = \alpha_i \frac{f(z)}{z_i};$$

this implies that all marginal productivities are positive if and only if all inputs are positive.

It is clear that substitution among all inputs is always possible with Cobb–Douglas production functions, provided that all inputs are taken as being in positive quantities. On every level curve of f the **rate of substitution** between inputs i, j, denoted by s_{ij}, all other inputs held constant, is defined by the formula

$$s_{ij} = dz_i/dz_j = -\alpha_j z_i/(\alpha_i z_j).$$

The value assumed by a rate of substitution is not independent of the units chosen to measure inputs; thus, a formula that better expresses the intensity of substitution between pairs of inputs is the so called **elasticity of substitution**, defined along any given level curve of f by the formula

$$\sigma_{ij} = \frac{d\ln(z_i/z_j)}{d\ln(f_j/f_i)}, \tag{2.2}$$

which does not depend on measuring units. If we write $f_i dz_i + f_j dz_j = 0$, because output is held constant along a level curve, together with all inputs other than i, j, performing the differentials in the preceding formula one obtains: $\sigma_{ij} = \sigma_{ji} = 1$, for all pairs i, j, independently of the values taken by the parameters of the Cobb–Douglas function.

3.3 CES Production Functions

A generalization of the Cobb–Douglas function is the so called **CES production function** proposed by Arrow et al. (1961). Using the previous notations it is written as

$$z \mapsto f(z) = a \left(\sum_i \alpha_i z_i^\beta \right)^{1/\beta}, \tag{3.1}$$

for $\beta \neq 0$. It is possible to verify that a CES function becomes a Cobb–Douglas function in the case that we have $\beta = 0$. Applying the elasticity formula (2.2) to any pair of inputs we find, for all input pairs,

$$\sigma_{ij} = \frac{1}{1 - \beta} \qquad (\beta \neq 1).$$

In contrast to a Cobb–Douglas production function, the level curves of a CES function can be convex or concave to the origin. E.g., let us take $\beta = -1$; then function (3.1) becomes:

$$f(z) = \frac{a}{\sum_i(\alpha_i/z_i)};$$

its level curves are branches of hyperbolae in the non-negative orthant of $\Re^n$, whose asymptotes are parallel to the coordinate axes, as shown by the following Figure 3.2.

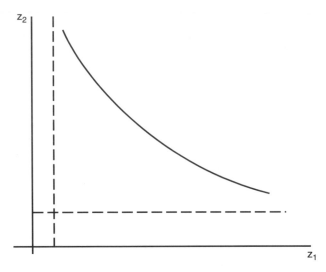

Fig. 3.2. A CES Level Curve ($\beta = -1$)

When $\beta = 1$, a level curve of the CES production function is represented by a segment of a straight line, shown in Figure 3.3, while if $\beta = 2$ the level curve of CES looks as in Figure 3.4.

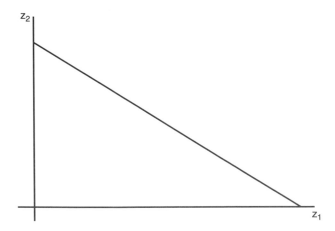

Fig. 3.3. A CES Level Curve ($\beta = 1$)

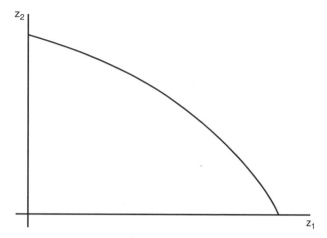

Fig. 3.4. A CES Level Curve ($\beta = 2$)

From Figures 3.2–3.4 it can be seen that CES functions are much more flexible than Cobb–Douglas ones. Of course, (3.1) has constant returns to scale, but it is straightforward to multiply the exponent, $1/\beta$, by a positive constant r, i.e. to write r/β as an exponent, to obtain a positively homogeneous production function of degree r. A possibly negative property of CES functions, not shared by Cobb–Douglas functions, is that the marginal productivity of input h can be positive even when all other inputs are zero; indeed we have

$$f_h(z) = a \left(\sum_i \alpha_i z_i^\beta \right)^{1/\beta - 1} \alpha_h z_h^{\beta - 1},$$

which is equal to $a\alpha_h^{1/\beta}$ when $z_j = 0$ for every $j \neq h$.

3.4 Leontief Production Functions

The fixed coefficients or Leontief production function, using the above notations, is:

$$z \mapsto f(z) = a \min\{\alpha_1 z_1, \alpha_2 z_2, \ldots, \alpha_n z_n\}. \tag{4.1}$$

Its level curves are degenerate, in the sense that instead of being strictly decreasing they possess an L form, whose sides are parallel to the axes:

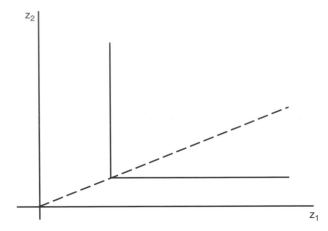

Fig. 3.5. A Leontief Level Curve

Of course, this means that there is no efficient possibility of substitution among inputs, and the only efficient technology in every level curve is the one corresponding to its vertex; the straight dashed line corresponds to the equation $z_2 = (\alpha_1/\alpha_2)z_1$. It should be pointed out that this production function is only of historical interest, since in real world economies every commodity can be produced at least by a finite set of production techniques; moreover, as we shall see from the computer experiments, the time paths of the main variables change in response to the changes in the parameters α_js.[2]

It might be of interest to recall that a Leontief function can be seen as a limiting case of a CES function, obtained for $\beta \to -\infty$. This property, once more, shows the flexibility of the family of CES functions with constant returns to scale.

3.5 Remainder

All the computer experiments in the succeeding chapters are tailored to these three functions. Of course, many other types of production functions have been proposed, at both the theoretical and applied levels, but for our purposes we consider these three functions suffice to illustrate the proposed simulations.

---

[2] This is a very serious error; economic statistics are not very accurate, even today.

Part II

Simple Dynamic Macromodels

4

A Model Without R&D and Public Expenditure

4.1 Introduction

Starting from Solow's (1956) theoretical macromodel, summarized in Chapter 1, which was applied to analyse some of the main determinants of economic growth, a large literature has been devoted to the grand theme of the time evolution of an economy, and of its business cycles.[1] In this chapter we focus on one element contributing to economic growth, and to business cycles, that is often not considered explicitly in general theoretical macromodels: this is the working of the labour market. Of course, a number of papers have tried to analyse the dynamic macromodels capable of generating steady growth and/or cyclic time paths, e.g. Goodwin (1967), Gabisch and Lorenz (1987, Ch. 5), Matsuyama (1999) and his references, but none of these papers explicitly introduces the labour market as a possible cause of business cycles.[2]

Formal analysis of the model, expressed by the system of two difference equations (2.11) and (2.12) below, is somewhat difficult, because of the number of cases that need to be taken into consideration. In Part 3, a number of computer simulations are implemented to provide a concrete picture of the various possibilities that apply to the time paths of the main variables.[3]

---

[1] For a good presentation of many dynamic macromodels, and micro-founded macromodels, the book by Azariadis (1993) is very useful; see also Allen (1967) for a clear exposition of some older models.

[2] Here we consider specifically endogenously generated business cycles.

[3] In a sense, for present day economists computer simulations are a modern version of the "thought experiments" familiar to physicists since the time of Galileo. This point is very well documented by Miller (1996).

4.2 The Macro Model

The notations are the customary ones: Y_t denotes total production, i.e. GDP, obtained at the end of period t, C_t is total consumption in period t, K_t is total capital at the start of period t, I_t is total investment.

To consider the labour market in its most basic elements,[4] we introduce three new variables: X_t denotes generically a quantity of labour (demanded or supplied) in period t, while L_t stands for the amount of labour supplied by the set of families, and N_t means the amount of labour demanded by firms. E_t is the effective quantity of labour employed by the production sector, i.e. $E_t = \min\{L_t, N_t\}$, the minimum between supply and demand.

Because there is only one (composite) commodity, it is always possible to assume it is chosen as numeraire, thus its price is $p_t = 1$ for every t; then w_t denotes both the real and the nominal wage rate in period t.

Based on the previous symbols it is possible to write the relations of the dynamic model. If $F : \Re_+^2 \to \Re_+$ denotes the economy-wide production function, summarizing the set of technologies known by the sector of firms, the first relation is the customary production function:

$$Y_{t+1} = F(K_t, X_t), \tag{2.1}$$

i.e., the end of period t maximum output, gross of capital depreciation, is obtained from the amounts of capital and of labour applied to production at the start of the period.

The second relation affects consumption. Here we do not consider any representative agent, but simply assume that only active workers consume, and that they consume, period after period, their whole labour income, making no allowance for leisure time. Assuming wages are paid at the end of every period, we have

$$C_t = w_{t-1}X_{t-1}. \tag{2.2}$$

Of course, this amounts to assuming that only workers that are employed receive an income. Relation (2.2) should be compared to the usual Keynesian consumption function, according to which consumption is an increasing function[5] of total production (i.e. income). Note that by choosing consumption this way, according to the next relations (2.5) and (2.7), the savings rate, i.e.

$$s_t = (Y_t - C_t)/Y_t = I_t/Y_t = \pi_{t-1}/Y_t, \tag{2.3}$$

becomes an endogenous variable, while in the Solow–Swan model it is an exogenous constant.[6] We can say that here the overall savings rate is a variable

---

[4] The same type of model, but with time considered as a continuous variable, is studied and implemented by Nicola (2004).

[5] Usually a proper fraction.

[6] See Barro and Sala-i-Martin (2004: Ch. 2), for a cogent argument on the importance of having the savings rate determined endogenously. The authors consider either a utility maximizing consumer, whose life extends indefinitely into the future, or overlapping generations of consumers.

quantity, because capitalists save all their profit income while workers consume all their labour income.

The next relation is the usual dynamic one, for the accumulation of total capital:

$$K_{t+1} + C_{t+1} = F(K_t, X_t) + (1 - \delta)K_t, \tag{2.4}$$

where δ, verifying $0 < \delta < 1$, is the rate of capital decay, and K_t is the quantity of capital at the start of period t. As capital is partly fixed capital and partly circulating capital, δ is never equal either to zero or to one.

Next we consider the set of firms as if they were a single firm acting as a pure competitor. Assuming that capital is permanently and totally owned by firms, total profit, π_t, is given by $\pi_t = Y_{t+1} - w_t X_t$, i.e.

$$\pi_t = F(K_t, X_t) - w_t X_t. \tag{2.5}$$

In this formula π_t ought to mean expected profit in period t; but, as the output price equals 1 in all periods, π_t also measures the effective profit obtained in period t.

For given values of K_t and w_t, when F is chosen to be of class C^2, the optimal quantity of labour demanded by firms is obtained by the relation:

$$\frac{\partial \pi_t}{\partial X_t} = \frac{\partial F(K_t, X_t)}{\partial X_t} - w_t = 0.$$

Making the usual assumption that both marginal productivities of F are positive, and moreover that $\frac{\partial^2 F}{\partial X^2} = F_{XX} < 0$ always, we can invert the previous equality, substituting N_t for X_t to mean the optimal quantity of labour chosen by firms, and obtain

$$N_t = F_X^{-1}(w_t; K_t), \tag{2.6}$$

i.e. the optimal amount of labour demanded by firms is a decreasing function of the wage rate, due to the assumption $F_{XX} < 0$, for every positive amount of capital. Moreover, when useful we can add to F the Inada conditions reported in Section 3 of Chapter 2.

Inserting (2.6) into production function (2.1), and profit function (2.5), we obtain the "first best" GDP, and the "first best" maximum profit,[7] corresponding to all possible pairs K_t, w_t, respectively

$$Y_{t+1} = F(K_t, N_t), \qquad \pi_t = F(K_t, N_t) - w_t N_t.$$

By assuming F to be positively homogeneous to the first degree (i.e. constant returns to scale), we have that $F(K, X) = F_K K + F_X X$, based on $F_K = \frac{\partial F}{\partial K}$, and $F_X = \frac{\partial F}{\partial X}$. But, in equilibrium $F_X(K_t, N_t) = w_t$ is true; so we have that $\pi_t = K_t F_K(K_t, X_t)$ and profit is positive for all values of X_t, and not only when the labour demand is N_t.

---

[7] I.e., the values obtained when there is no constraint on the optimal quantity of labour demanded by firms.

Previously it was assumed that all labour income is consumed; now we make the assumption that all profits are invested.[8] Thus the following relation becomes part of the model:

$$I_t = \pi_{t-1}, \tag{2.7}$$

meaning that total profits in every period are invested in the next period.

Relations (2.2) and (2.7) state that workers save nothing, while capitalists consume nothing; a more sensible way to consider consumption (and savings) is based on the seminal contribution of Kaldor (1956, pp. 94–100), which assumes that both workers and capitalists save a fraction of their incomes.[9]

From relations (2.2), (2.5) with E_t replacing X_t and N_t, and (2.7), we have

$$Y_t = C_t + I_t,$$

or the customary accounting identity[10] between resources existing at the start of period t and how they are employed by consumers and by firms.

In passing, it should be mentioned that substituting the last equality into (2.4) we obtain $K_{t+1} = I_{t+1} + (1 - \delta)K_t$.

Let us now consider labour supply, which comes from families. In economic terms, we can assume that the amount supplied is a function of the wage rate only; so we can write

$$L_t = g_c(w_t), \tag{2.8}$$

where g_c is the function (2.1) in Chapter 2, which takes on positive values when the wage rate is greater than the minimum wage rate, $\underline{w} > 0$. Hence, the amount of labour hired by firms is

$$E_t = \min\{N_t, L_t\}. \tag{2.9}$$

We must add a difference equation for the choice of the wage rate in every time period; assuming there is some meta-agent, such as a Walrasian auctioneer, we can write

$$w_{t+1} = w_t \phi(N_t, L_t), \tag{2.10}$$

where $\phi : \Re_+^2 \to \Re_+$ is a strictly increasing function of N, and a strictly decreasing function of L.[11] In the Internet age, one can assume that the wage rate is adjusted, in every time period, by means of an electronic auction between the set of firms and the set of families.

The simplified model is formed by equations (2.1)–(2.10), two of which, i.e. (2.4) and (2.10), form a non-linear system of first order finite difference

---

[8] Capitalists are pure spirits!
[9] See also Pasinetti (1962).
[10] Walras's law applied to this type of model.
[11] But see Solow (1990, Ch. 3), which convincingly argues against the possibility of fixing the wage rate by trying to equalize demand and supply.

equations. After substituting the other relations of the model into (2.4) and (2.10), the difference equation system looks as follows:

$$K_{t+1} = (1 - \delta)K_t + F[K_t, \min\{F_X^{-1}(w_t; K_t), g_c(w_t)\}]+ \tag{2.11}$$

$$-w_t \min\{F_X^{-1}(w_t; K_t), g_c(w_t)\},$$

$$w_{t+1} = w_t \phi[F_X^{-1}(w_t; K_t), g_c(w_t)]. \tag{2.12}$$

The existence of a stationary equilibrium, i.e., a pair of positive values such that $K_t = \hat{K}$ and $w_t = \hat{w}$ for all values of t, is a solution to the pair of non-linear equations

$$F[K, \min\{F_X^{-1}(w; K), g_c(w)\}] + (1-\delta)K = w \min\{F_X^{-1}(w; K), g_c(w)\}, \tag{2.13}$$

$$\phi[F_X^{-1}(w; K), g_c(w)] = 1. \tag{2.14}$$

When labour supply is a continuous function of the real wage rate, whose values belong to the interval $[0, \bar{L}]$, as in Figure 2 in Chapter 2, while for every K labour demand is a decreasing function of w, equation (2.14) has up to three solutions, corresponding to every positive K.[12] Let $w = \psi(K)$ denote any one of these values; substitution into (2.13) yields an equation only in K, whose solutions determine the possible values taken by capital at a stationary equilibrium. Let us define $\Psi(K) = g_c[\psi(K)]$, to be inserted in the difference equation (2.11); then this equation becomes:

$$K_{t+1} = (1 - \delta)K_t + F[K_t, \min\{F_X^{-1}[\psi(K_t); K_t], \Psi(K_t)\}]+ \tag{2.15}$$

$$-\psi(K_t) \min\{F_X^{-1}[\psi(K_t); K_t], \Psi(K_t)\}.$$

At this level of generality it would seem difficult to study the dynamic behaviour of equation (2.15); thus, in the following section, we introduce specific functions.

4.3 Choice of Functions to Implement the Model

It is not our aim to consider the existence of a solutions problem in its generality; we are mainly interested in presenting computer simulations, our "thought experiments", implemented by means of specific functions, to show the richness of the possible time paths followed by the main variables in this model economy. So, let us now consider the production functions presented in Chapter 3, which will be employed in the numeric simulations implemented in Part 3, and the labour market supply function.

---

[12] See Figure 4 in Ch. 2.

4.3.1 Cobb–Douglas Production Function

The customary constant returns to scale Cobb–Douglas function, presented in Chapter 3, given β satisfying $0 < \beta < 1$, and $\theta > 0$, is:

$$F(K, X) = \theta K^\beta X^{1-\beta}; \tag{3.1}$$

since we have $F_X = (1 - \beta)\theta K^\beta X^{-\beta}$, relation (2.6) is

$$N_t = [\theta(1 - \beta)]^{1/\beta} \frac{K_t}{w_t^{1/\beta}}. \tag{3.2}$$

Parameter θ is a productivity parameter that is especially useful when considering technical progress.

4.3.2 CES Production Function

A second type of production function we consider in the computer simulations is the constant returns to scale CES production function. According to formula (3.1) in Chapter 3, for $\beta \neq 0, a > 0, b > 0$, it can be written as:

$$F(K, X) = \theta(aK^\beta + bX^\beta)^{1/\beta}, \tag{3.3}$$

and in this case in place of (3.2) the optimal labour input for the set of firms is:

$$N_t = \frac{a^{1/\beta} K_t}{[(\frac{w_t}{b\theta})^{\frac{\beta}{1-\beta}} - b]^{1/\beta}} \qquad (\beta \neq 0, \beta \neq 1). \tag{3.4}$$

Since N_t has to be positive, and the numerator in this formula is always positive, the wage rate must render the denominator positive, i.e., the wage rate must satisfy $w_t > \theta b^{1/\beta}$ for every t, when β is positive, and the reversed inequality when β is negative. Moreover, for N_t to maximize profit, one must have $\pi_{XX} < 0$, and this is true only for $\beta \in (-\infty, 1)$.

4.3.3 Leontief Technology

The third type is a Leontief production function, which also was introduced in Chapter 3. Here, it can be written as

$$F(K, X) = \theta \min\{aK, bX\}, \tag{3.5}$$

for θ, a, b positive parameters. Since we have chosen as numeraire the price of output, parameter b is the value of one unit of labour input. Labour demand, then, is based on the comparison between θb and w. Indeed, given $K > 0$, if $\min\{aK, bX\} = bX$ then the profit is $\pi = \theta bX - wX = (\theta b - w)X$, which is positive only for $\theta b > w$, while if $\min\{aK, bX\} = aK$ then we have $\pi = \theta aK - wX < \theta bX - wX = (\theta b - w)X$, which is negative when $\theta b < w$.

Since it is unprofitable to hire labour input greater than is required, given K_t the demand for labour for the Leontief technology is:

$$N_t = \frac{a}{b} K_t \qquad (\theta b > w_t), \qquad (3.6)$$

where $\pi_t = (\theta b - w_t)(a/b)K_t = a(\theta - w_t/b)K_t$. In the reverse case, i.e. for $\theta b \leq w_t$, then either $\pi_t = 0$, or $\pi_t = \theta aK_t - w_t(a/b)K_t = a(\theta - w_t/b)K_t$ whenever this quantity is positive, which occurs again for $\theta b > w_t$. To summarize, either (3.6) is true, or $N_t = 0$.

4.3.4 Labour Supply

With respect to the labour supply, let us consider the assumption referred to in Chapter 2, that the amount of labour supplied by families is an increasing function of the wage rate for low and for high values of w, while it is decreasing in between. As explained in Chapter 2, an explanation of this phenomenon is that at low levels of w the supply of labour increases because there is an incentive to work harder in order to get a more satisfactory income; but then a point is reached where income is sufficiently abundant to induce a reduction in the labour supply in favour of leisure time (an income effect). At even higher values of w there is again a strong incentive to increase the supply of labour.[13] Perhaps, this phenomenon can be explained at the family level, when, e.g., there are three people of working age: at low levels of w both husband and wife are compelled to work, but when w is sufficiently high only the husband works (and the son/daughter is in higher education). Thereafter w becomes so high (i.e. so rewarding) as to induce all three of these family members to become part of the work force.[14] A cubic equation, such as presented in Chapter 2, is adequate here:

$$L_t = \min\left\{\bar{L}, \max\{0, -a_0 + a_1 w_t - a_2 w_t^2 + a_3 w_t^3\}\right\}. \qquad (3.7)$$

Function (3.7) is depicted in Figure 2 of Chapter 2. One point should be mentioned: that the wage rate could be, or could become, so low that the supply of labour is zero. Then employment and output become zero; wages and consumption, and profits and investments, will also be zero. In such a case, the whole economy ceases to exist, except for capital, whose difference equation (2.4) now becomes $K_{t+1} = (1 - \delta)K_t$, i.e. capital continuously decreases to zero, the value obtained from $t \to \infty$. Of course, this state of affairs is economically rather uninteresting.

---

[13] This fact, as argued by Solow (1990, p. 3), makes the labour market quite distinct from all other markets.

[14] See also the Appendix, which elaborates on this point.

The next function is ϕ; considering a positive parameter α, verifying $0 < \alpha < 1$, we can write:

$$\phi(N, L) = 1 + \alpha \frac{N - L}{L},$$

and correspondingly

$$w_{t+1} = w_t \left(1 + \alpha \frac{N_t - L_t}{L_t} \right). \tag{3.8}$$

Of course, this equation mimics the action of a Walrasian auctioneer. The choice of this function is made to render the two sides of (3.8) dimensionally homogeneous; indeed, considering α as a pure number measuring the adjustment velocity of the wage rate, both sides of (3.8) have the dimension of the wage rate. It is also possible to write (3.8) as follows:

$$w_{t+1} = w_t \left[\frac{\alpha N_t + (1 - \alpha) L_t}{L_t} \right],$$

to show that the wage adjusting equation (3.8) can be seen as a convex combination of labour demand and labour supply.

This completes the specification of all the functions required to allow us, in Part 3, to implement some numerical simulations when the production function is of a Cobb–Douglas, a CES, or a Leontief type.

With respect to labour, we consider labour supply function (3.7), of the reversed S type, under three possible situations: a stationary population, a population growing at a steady rate, and a population growing according to logistic law.

5
Some Determinants of Endogenous Growth

5.1 Introduction

In Chapter 4 it was assumed that income, Y, in every period is split into two parts, consumption, C, and gross investment, I. In the real world quite frequently a fraction of income is neither consumed nor directly invested in production, but is invested indirectly in production, i.e. it is devoted to R&D to improve the productivity of inputs directly entering production.[1] Here we want to extend the model presented in Chapter 4 to include the expenditure on R&D, denoted by R, so that the basic relation among aggregate quantities will be the sum of three components, $Y = C + I + R$.

5.2 Expenditure on R&D

The simplified version of the model presented in Chapter 4, does not include expenditure on R&D. Of course, at least in the so called rich countries, every year some fraction, let us say from 1% to 3%, of GDP is devoted to improvements to existing production techniques, or even to inventing new goods (and thus new technologies for their production).[2] In the early decades of the 20th century the Austrian economist Schumpeter (1912) introduced the notion of the "innovating entrepreneur", which he described as a producer ready to experiment in his firm, on the introduction of new goods and new technologies.[3]

---

[1] On R&D activity and technological progress see, among others, Romer (1987, 1990), Grossman and Helpman (1991), Aghion and Howitt (1992). See also Part I in Hornung (2002).

[2] Sometimes, some serendipitous event allows technology to improve without any direct R&D effort; but the probabilities of this occurring are low.

[3] Of course, in a macroeconomic model it is impossible to introduce new commodities, since all goods are aggregated into one composite commodity; what is possible is to introduce new technologies.

As Schumpeter predicted, the main problem for an innovator is the need to raise financial backing for his new production activities; Schumpeter regarded this type of funding to be one of the main tasks of the banking system, which, in his day as also today, is not very ready to lend to innovators. Here we ignore this problem,[4] but we suppose that whatever funds are needed to innovate, they are at the disposal of the production sphere of the economy, since they are financed totally out of profits.

The model we are proposing introduces R&D expenditure in a simple and direct way. It is customary, in applied analyses, to consider annual expenditure on R&D as a percentage of GDP. This is the correct way to consider this type of expenditure, because the greater part of it comes from governments, and only a relatively small percentage comes from firms. But, here, GDP is split into two parts, wages and profits; thus, in our model, R&D expenditure must come out of profits. In the present work R&D activity is considered to be a percentage of the profits accruing to firms in the previous year. Therefore, let us assume that in every period profits are partly deemed not to accrue directly to the stock of capital, but to increase the total productivity of the production subsystem. Let us take R_t to denote the expenditure on R&D in period t, with I_t denoting the usual investment. Thus, for every t we must have the accounting identity

$$Y_t = C_t + I_t + R_t. \tag{2.1}$$

Since, as Chapter 4 showed, total investment, $I_t + R_t$, equals the total profits of the producing sector, we have $I_t + R_t = \pi_{t-1}$.

5.3 Endogenous Technical Progress

For the purposes of this chapter, it is useful from the start to introduce into the production function, F, a multiplicative parameter, $\theta_t(t = 1, 2, 3, \ldots)$, as a measure of the total productivity index of the economy in period t; i.e., for given positive values of θ_t, K_t, X_t, the expression $\theta_t F(K_t, X_t)$ denotes the maximum possible output in period t. This amounts to assuming that technical progress applies equally to both inputs, capital and labour, i.e., that technical progress is of the so called disembodied type.[5]

---

[4] See Aghion and Howitt (1998) in discussing some macroeconomic models relating to innovating firms. It is the opinion of this author that the primary purpose of macroeconomic models is to provide insights to increase understanding of the main determinants of growth and cycles, without going into huge detail.

[5] Technological progress, as expressed by the function $\theta_t F(K_t, X_t)$, is referred to as *Hicks neutral* (Hicks 1932). It is accepted that technical progress can be embodied in labour or in capital, or in both. Very frequently, when considering technical progress in labour, which amounts to **producing** skilled labour from unskilled labour, it is customary to refer to skilled labour as **human capital**; in the opin-

Let us assume that the expenditure R_t is devoted to paying the wages of workers employed in R&D activity in firms, labour being the only input necessary to produce new knowledge, which becomes totally incorporated in the sequence of values taken by θ_t. Of course, in real world economies, R&D workers are usually much more highly qualified (trained) than the average worker engaged in material production activity; thus, their wage rates are proportionally higher than those of other workers. However, here we ignore this fact and suppose that the same wage rate, w_t, applies to both types of workers.

From now on, we use X_t^p to denote the period t labour input into production, and X_t^r to denote the period t labour input into R&D activity. Moreover, let $f : \Re_+ \to \Re_+$ be the **R&D production function**, such that $f(X^r)$ is the increment in the total productivity parameter resulting from applying the labour input X^r to R&D activity. More specifically, let us assume

$$\theta_{t+1} = \theta_t + f(X_t^r),$$

for every $t = 1, 2, 3, \ldots.$. Of course, f is considered to have all the good properties associated with every respectable production function: it confirms $f(0) = 0$, it is differentiable as many times as needed, its first derivative is positive, i.e. $f'(X) > 0$ everywhere, and its second derivative is negative, or $f''(X) < 0$, i.e. R&D activity always shows positive productivity, but returns to scale are decreasing.[6]

Since, as already noted, labour input is now employed in two distinct activities, production of material commodities and R&D activity, total labour input, X_t, is expressed by $X_t = X_t^p + X_t^r$ for every t. Let us assume that in every period, firms aim at maximizing their profits from material production, expressed by the formula

$$\pi_t = \theta_t F(K_t, X_t^p) - w_t X_t^p, \tag{3.1}$$

as only X_t^p is devoted to immediate production; X_t^r is actually devoted to future production, since it raises the value of θ in the next time period. By

---

ion of this author this usage of the word capital is very damaging when applied to labour, because in some sense the term human capital assimilates persons (labour) with things (capital). Some interesting models in which technical progress comes from skilled labour, i.e. from R&D activity devoted to training labour, are proposed by Lucas (1988), and by Uzawa (1965). See also the monograph by Quadrio Curzio (1971).

[6] This way of describing R&D is rather naive; e.g., Rivera-Batiz and Romer (1991), and Matsuyama (1999) are much more elaborate on this point. But here it is argued that in a macromodel, where every variable is the result of a deep process of aggregation, the previous equation is sufficient to render the process of endogenous technical progress. Moreover, in Matsuyama's model cycles are of the simple cobweb type, and thus look quite different from the business cycles observed in real world economies.

maximizing function (3.1), under the usual regularity conditions on F, the optimal labour demand is

$$N_t^p = F_X^{-1}(w_t/\theta_t; K_t). \tag{3.2}$$

Inserting this function into π_t we have

$$\pi_t = \theta_t F[K_t, F_X^{-1}(w_t/\theta_t; K_t)] - w_t F_X^{-1}(w_t/\theta_t; K_t), \tag{3.3}$$

to be considered as the first best profit since, due to the possibility of rationing in the labour market, it is possible that firms cannot hire the optimal labour input needed.

Given the parameter ϵ, satisfying $0 < \epsilon < 1$, let us assume that the following relation holds true for all time periods:

$$R_t = \epsilon \max\{0, \pi_{t-1}\}, \tag{3.4}$$

i.e., when profits are positive, the fraction, ϵ, of total profits in any period is devoted to R&D in the following period; it is constant in time and fixed exogenously.[7] Here, to simplify the simulations, we have chosen to consider the expenditure on R&D as a proper fraction of profits, rather than a fraction of GDP. In applied economics profits are usually a fixed percentage of GDP, but there is no loss of generality in our choice; it is only a question of choosing the appropriate value to be assigned to ϵ, which must be comparatively greater when applied to profits than to GDP, in order to determine R&D expenditure.

Once R_t is given, labour input into R&D activity must satisfy the relation $w_t X_t^r = R_t$, i.e., the quantity of labour demanded by firms for R&D activity is

$$N_t^r = R_t/w_t.$$

Thus, firms' total labour demand is $N_t = N_t^p + N_t^r$, or

$$N_t = F_X^{-1}(w_t/\theta_t; K_t) + R_t/w_t. \tag{3.5}$$

Given N_t^r, we obtain $\theta_{t+1} = \theta_t + f(N_t^r)$. By inserting (3.3) and (3.4) into this relation, we can write

$$\begin{aligned}
\theta_{t+1} = \theta_t + f[\epsilon \max\{0, \theta_{t-1} F[K_{t-1}, F_X^{-1}(w_{t-1}/\theta_{t-1}; K_{t-1})] + \\
- w_{t-1} F_X^{-1}(w_{t-1}/\theta_{t-1}; K_{t-1})\}/w_t].
\end{aligned} \tag{3.6}$$

Clearly, (3.6) is a third difference equation to be added to the two difference equations in Chapter 4.

Specific consideration of (3.6) is in order. While output is almost always a sure result of production, the resources applied to R&D generally give only expected results, with some positive probability which is less than unity; this

---

[7] Of course, it is possible to endogenize how this fraction is chosen by the set of firms.

fact needs to be incorporated into equation (3.6). For example, if q is the (positive) probability that $f(X^r)$ really improves the total productivity parameter, one could multiply $f(X^r)$ by 1 when R&D is successful (with probability q), and by 0 when R&D is not successful (with probability $1 - q$). On average, i.e. when considering a sufficiently long time range, this amounts to multiplying $f(X^r)$ by the quantity q; hence, in formula (3.6) we are allowed to think of the value taken by $f(X^r)$ as already incorporating the coefficient expressing the probability of success in R&D.

Total optimal labour demand by firms, $N_t = N_t^p + N_t^r$, can be compared to labour supply by families, expressed by $L_t = g_c(w_t)$. Thus, effective employment is expressed by $E_t = \min\{N_t, g_c(w_t)\}$; when firms are rationed in the labour market, because $g_c(w_t) < N_t$, let us assume that effective labour employed by firms is, respectively:

$$E_t^p = (N_t^p/N_t)g_c(w_t), \qquad E_t^r = (N_t^r/N_t)g_c(w_t). \qquad (3.7)$$

In other words, labour employed in the two activities is proportional to the two optimal labour demands; of course we have $E_t = E_t^p + E_t^r$. Thus, total effective consumption is $C_t = w_{t-1}E_{t-1}$ and profits become second best profits, which are obtained by substituting, in formula (3.3), the value E_t^p to N_t^p. In the same way, R_t too is determined by the second best profit. Accordingly, formula (3.6) becomes:

$$\theta_{t+1} = \theta_t + f\left[\epsilon \max\{0, \theta_{t-1}F(K_{t-1}, E_{t-1}^p) - w_{t-1}E_{t-1}^p\}/w_t\right]. \qquad (3.8)$$

Thanks to the total productivity dynamics expressed by this equation, the economy is no longer an economy operating under stationary conditions; it is capable of becoming a progressive economy. But this is no more the consequence of an exogenously increasing labour force, as in Solow's model, which was summarized in Chapter 1, or of exogenous technical progress; presently, it is due to the increased total productivity induced by the endogenous technical progress generated by R&D activity.

The previous relations are added to the dynamic model presented in Chapter 4; the enlarged model now includes three first order difference equations, in the variables K, w, θ. They are:

$$K_{t+1} = (1 - \delta)K_t + \theta_t F(K_t, E_t^p) - w_t E_t - R_{t+1}, \qquad (3.9)$$

$$w_{t+1} = w_t\phi[F_X^{-1}(w_t/\theta_t; K_t) + R_t/w_t, g_c(w_t)], \qquad (3.10)$$

$$\theta_{t+1} = \theta_t + f\left[\epsilon/w_t \max\{0, \theta_{t-1}F(K_{t-1}, E_{t-1}^p) - w_{t-1}E_{t-1}^p\}\right]. \qquad (3.11)$$

In formulae (3.9) and (3.11), to simplify the notations we have retained the symbols E_t^p and E_t, but it should be understood that they are a shorthand for formulae (3.2)–(3.5), and (3.7), so that the only variables in system (3.9)–(3.11) are the state variables K, w, θ.

5.4 Choice of Functions for the Simulations

Based on the specific functions F, f, g_c, and ϕ, in Part 3 we consider a number of computer simulations. Functions F, g_c, and ϕ will be as in Chapter 4, while for f we consider the function

$$X^r \mapsto f(X^r) = c(X^r)^d, \tag{4.1}$$

where c and d are positive parameters, and $0 < d < 1$. This choice of f means, of course, that we are assuming there are positive, but decreasing returns to R&D activity. Moreover, by choosing $c < 1$, in some sense we are taking account of the fact that the probability of R&D efforts being successful is less than 1.

6

Public Expenditure and Taxes

6.1 Introduction

The models in Chapters 4 and 5 do not consider that in all present day economies – even non-centrally managed ones – governments intervene heavily in the economic sphere. On the one hand governments raise taxes from citizens and firms, while on the other they supply public goods which very often, but not always, are essential to everyday economic activity. By way of example, we can mention the supply of services such as education, public health, justice,[1] national defence, and the supply of goods such as infrastructures, from roads to railways to airports, and public utilities, from water to electricity to gas supply.

The macromodel aims at including government expenditure, its financing from the taxes that can be levied on wages and profits, and the production of public goods. Since we are not considering money, or its substitutes, the government budget is assumed always to be balanced, i.e. in every period it is assumed that expenditure equals receipts.

6.2 Modelling Taxes and Public Expenditure

Denoting T_t as the amount of taxes collected from agents in period t, and G_t as the corresponding public expenditure, the assumption in the balanced budget in every period is simply written[2] as

---

[1] E.g., to regulate and enforce contracts in the economy.

[2] As an alternative to this possibility, and assuming that the government is constrained only to spend at most all the taxes, we could substitute the above equation with this one: $\sum_{t=1}^{t^*} T_t \leq \sum_{t=1}^{t^*} G_t$ for every t^*. Were the government able to assess carefully the impact of public expenditure on the production sphere, this way of considering the government budget could allow public authorities to try to maximize GDP along some given time horizon, e.g., by choosing a counter

$$G_t = T_t. \tag{2.1}$$

A drastic and very simplified way to introduce taxes is to assume that there is no fiscal imposition on wages, and that there is a fixed rate, τ, verifying $0 < \tau < 1$, to tax profits, π, which is constant over time. Then we have

$$T_t = \tau \pi_{t-1} \tag{2.2}$$

generally, for period t taxes are levied on the previous period's profits. According to (2.1) and (2.2), period t public expenditure is expressed by

$$G_t = \tau \pi_{t-1}. \tag{2.3}$$

At the macroeconomic level, public expenditure has a direct impact on the production side of the economy, in the sense that it raises, ceteris paribus, the productivity of labour and capital.[3] Let us refer generically to **infrastructure** as the output of public expenditure; we assume that infrastructure is a non-decaying input, i.e. it accumulates fully from period to period, and use Z_t to denote the amount of infrastructure at the disposal of the economy at the start of period t. Let us also assume that every unit of public expenditure, G, generates a fraction κ of infrastructure, Z, by means of the ad hoc "production function", $G \mapsto \kappa G$;[4] thus, at the start of every period t the quantity of infrastructure is

$$Z_t = Z_{t-1} + \kappa G_{t-1}. \tag{2.4}$$

6.3 The Production Sector of the Economy

Once infrastructure has been introduced as an input, the production function, F, has three arguments: labour, X, capital, K, and infrastructure, Z, i.e., $(K, X, Z) \mapsto F(K, X, Z)$ which is the maximum quantity, Y, that can be obtained by applying inputs K, X, Z to the production of GDP. This amounts to considering Z as a third factor of production, physically identical to K and Y.

Of course, it is reasonable and useful, in the production function, to apply to Z the same assumptions as made for the other two inputs, i.e.: $F_Z > 0$, or the marginal productivity of infrastructure is always positive, and $F_{ZZ} < 0$, or its marginal productivity is decreasing with increasing Z. Let us also continue

---

cyclical public expenditure, aimed at smoothing business cycles, increasing public expenditure during periods of recession and decreasing it in economic booms. Since this would be rather difficult to estimate, the model in this chapter employs equation (2.1) as holding for all time periods.

[3] E.g., education aims, among others, to qualify the labour force, thereby increasing, ceteris paribus, its productivity.

[4] This assumption implies that there are constant returns to scale in the production of the infrastructure.

to assume F to be homogeneous to degree 1 in K and X, i.e., $F(\lambda K, \lambda X, Z) = \lambda F(K, X, Z)$ for all positive values λ and K, X, and for every positive Z. We can write the period t production function as

$$Y_{t+1} = \theta_t F(K_t, X_t, Z_t). \tag{3.1}$$

Before tax, profit is given by a similar formula to (3.1) in Chapter 5, i.e.

$$\pi_t = \theta_t F(K_t, X_t^p, Z_t) - w_t X_t^p, \tag{3.2}$$

while after tax, profit is

$$\pi_t^* = (1 - \tau)[\theta_t F(K_t, X_t^p, Z_t) - w_t X_t^p]. \tag{3.3}$$

It is π_t^* that the sector of firms aims at maximizing in every period; but because π_t^* is always proportional to π_t, given all other quantities the optimal demand for labour is still given by a relation similar to (3.2) in Chapter 5, or

$$N_t^p = F_X^{-1}(w_t/\theta_t; K_t, Z_t); \tag{3.4}$$

thus, we can rewrite (3.1)–(3.3) as follows:

$$Y_{t+1} = \theta_t F(K_t, N_t^p, Z_t), \tag{3.5}$$

$$\pi_t = \theta_t F(K_t, N_t^p, Z_t) - w_t N_t^p, \tag{3.6}$$

$$\pi_t^* = (1 - \tau)[\theta_t F(K_t, N_t^p, Z_t) - w_t N_t^p]. \tag{3.7}$$

6.4 A Macromodel with R&D and Public Expenditure

Many of the relations in the models presented in Chapters 4 and 5 are also contained in this model. Since firms can be constrained in their demand for labour by the supply from families, in equations (3.5)–(3.7) we substitute E_t^p for N_t^p, where E_t^p is determined by the following relation (4.10):

$$Y_{t+1} = \theta_t F(K_t, E_t^p, Z_t), \tag{4.1}$$

$$\pi_t = \theta_t F(K_t, E_t^p, Z_t) - w_t E_t^p, \tag{4.2}$$

$$\pi_t^* = (1 - \tau)[\theta_t F(K_t, E_t^p, Z_t) - w_t E_t^p]. \tag{4.3}$$

Equations (4.1)–(4.3), and (3.4) rewritten as

$$N_t^p = F_X^{-1}(w_t/\theta_t; K_t, Z_t), \tag{4.4}$$

are part of the present model. The other relations are formed by the equations in Chapters 4 and 5; for completeness in the presentation of the model, and assuming the meaning previously given to all symbols, let us add to (4.1)–(4.4) these other relations:[5]

$$R_t = \epsilon \max\{0, \pi_{t-1}^*\}, \tag{4.5}$$

$$N_t^r = R_t/w_t, \tag{4.6}$$

$$N_t = N_t^p + N_t^r, \tag{4.7}$$

$$L_t = g_c(w_t), \tag{4.8}$$

$$E_t = \min\{N_t, g_c(w_t)\}, \tag{4.9}$$

$$E_t^p = (N_t^p/N_t)E_t, \qquad E_t^r = (N_t^r/N_t)E_t, \tag{4.10}$$

$$C_t = w_{t-1}E_{t-1}, \tag{4.11}$$

$$K_{t+1} = (1-\delta)K_t + \theta_t F(K_t, E_t^p, Z_t) - w_t E_t - R_{t+1} - G_{t+1}, \tag{4.12}$$

$$w_{t+1} = w_t \phi(N_t, L_t), \tag{4.13}$$

$$\theta_{t+1} = \theta_t + f(E_t^r), \tag{4.14}$$

plus equation (2.4) for infrastructure, rewritten as

$$Z_{t+1} = Z_t + \kappa G_t. \tag{4.15}$$

If we consider that gross investment, I_{t+1}, is expressed by $I_{t+1} = K_{t+1} - (1-\delta)K_t$, from this relation and (4.12) we obtain the identity, i.e. Walras's law, for this macromodel,

$$Y_t = C_t + I_t + R_t + G_t$$

for every t. In other words, in every period GDP is split into four components: consumption, (private) gross investment, R&D expenditure, and public expenditure.

The dynamic equations of the model are (4.12)–(4.15). Substituting some of the other equations[6] into the first three we have:

$$K_{t+1} = (1-\delta)K_t + \theta_t F(K_t, E_t^p, Z_t) - w_t(E_t^p + E_t^r) - R_{t+1} - G_{t+1}, \tag{4.16}$$

$$w_{t+1} = w_t \phi[N_t^p + N_t^r, g_c(w_t)], \tag{4.17}$$

$$\theta_{t+1} = \theta_t + f(E_t^r). \tag{4.18}$$

---

[5] Note that relation (4.5) contains the preceding period's profit after tax, because now R&D expenditure comes out of the retained profit. Of course, in period t the value π_{t-1}^* is a given quantity.

[6] It seems unnecessary, and also cumbersome, to completely substitute all the equations (4.2)–(4.11) in order to write the dynamic system (4.15)–(4.18) in only four variables K, w, θ, Z.

6.5 Choosing the Functions for the Simulations

To conclude the presentation of the model, we need to specify the functions entering (4.16)–(4.18), which are needed to implement the simulations presented in Part 3. The functions in question are: g_c, ϕ, f and F; they are the same functions that were introduced with reference to the two preceding models, but for F, i.e.:

$$w_t \mapsto g_c(w_t) = \min\left\{\bar{L}, \max\{0, -a_0 + a_1 w_t - a_2 w_t^2 + a_3 w_t^3\}\right\}, \qquad (5.1)$$

$$(N_t, L_t) \mapsto \phi(N_t, L_t) = 1 + \alpha \frac{N_t - L_t}{L_t}, \qquad (5.2)$$

$$E_t^r \mapsto f(E_t^r) = c(E_t^r)^d, \qquad (5.3)$$

$$(K_t, X_t^p, Z_t) \mapsto F(K_t, X_t^p, Z_t) = \theta_t K_t^\beta (X_t^p)^{1-\beta} Z_t^\eta. \qquad (5.4)$$

Note that in (5.4) the usual Cobb–Douglas production function, considered in the previous chapters, is multiplied by Z_t^η, with $0 < \eta < 1$, meaning that we assume that there are decreasing returns in the accumulation of infrastructure. Moreover, constant returns to scale still prevail with reference to labour and capital. The choice of function (5.4) provides the possibility to compare the results obtained by simulating this model, when $Z_t = 1$ for all ts, with the corresponding results obtained when there is no public expenditure. In other words, by choosing $Z_0 = 1$ and $\tau = 0$, all the results obtained by implementing the present model are the same as those produced by the corresponding model with zero tax rate, zero public expenditure, and a constant amount of infrastructure, conventionally set equal to one unit.

Part III

Computer Simulations

The first three chapters of Part 3, i.e. Chapters 7–9, study the case of a stationary population (thus a stationary labour supply), when production functions are, respectively, of the Cobb–Douglas type, of the CES type, and of the Leontief type. Firstly, simulations are implemented when no R&D activity is present, and then when R&D expenditure is positive. In all cases no public expenditure is considered.

Then, limiting simulations to the case of Cobb–Douglas production functions, in Chapter 10 we examine what happens in the case of a steadily increasing population (and thus a steadily increasing labour force). The same types of simulations are implemented in Chapter 11 when population increases according to the logistic law. Again, no public expenditure is considered.

In Chapter 12, with reference to a stationary population and a Cobb–Douglas production function, we perform some simulations for the model containing both R&D expenditure and public expenditure.

Finally, in Chapter 13, as a measure of economic (material) welfare, we compute the undiscounted sum of consumptions in all periods, which, as explained in Section 2, Chapter 1, is considered to be an index of the economic welfare performance of the economy.

All simulations are implemented using MAPLE software, and the time horizon chosen is always $n = 120$. That is, we can assume that every period lasts one calendar month of time; thus, 120 periods cover a time interval of ten years, which time interval can be considered to be short enough, with reference to real economies, for all the parameters and functions of the models not to change significantly. But, to repeat an earlier caveat, it must be remembered that all the experiments presented here are thought experiments only, with no serious reference to any real situation.

Let us note in passing, that in many simulations the time paths of the economic variables look so complex that this in itself is evidence of the impossibility of solving analytically the models proposed in Part 2.

WARNING: all the simulations generate the same set of figures, numbered 1 to 16, but for every simulation only those figures that look interesting for the simulation in question are shown. This explains why, in many instances, figures generated by a simulation are not numbered consecutively, and sometimes their order does not respect the natural ordering of the integers. Moreover, in some simulations the time behaviour of the variables in the first (let us say 20) periods does not seem to agree with their behaviour in subsequent periods. This means that the starting values given to the state variables are economically unreasonable; thus, one can safely consider these time series from period 20 on, as if the starting values of the state variables were selected to be those holding in period 20.

7

Stationary Population:
Cobb–Douglas Simulations

7.1 Preliminary

Remembering that we have chosen to put $p_t = 1$ for all ts, where p_t denotes the price of the produced (composite) commodity, let us start by considering a stationary labour supply, and let us specify the values to be given to the parameters of the functions introduced in Chapter 2. The supply function of labour for all the simulations is

$$L_t = \min\left\{100, \max\{0, -6 + 30w_t - 8.1w_t^2 + 0.58w_t^3\}\right\},$$

i.e., we assume that only the real wage rate matters in choosing the amount of labour to be supplied by families. Of course, we always have $0 \le L_t \le 100$. The graphical representation of this function is similar to that in Figure 2 in Chapter 2.

Before considering the simulations, it is interesting to have an idea of the importance that the decay coefficient, or depreciation parameter, δ, has on the whole process of growth. Assuming the production function to be of a Cobb–Douglas type, let us consider the following parameter values: $\beta = 0.5$, $\theta = 6$, and take $\delta = 0.2$. Under these parameters the stationary values of the state variables are:

$$\hat{K} = 22500, \quad \hat{w} = 45.$$

Keeping all other parameter values constant, and changing only δ from 0.2 to 0.6 modifies the stationary values, which are now

$$\hat{K} = 2500, \quad \hat{w} = 15.$$

Choosing intermediate values for δ, it is easy to show quite clearly the sensitivity of the stationary values of the state variables, i.e. the values to which the economic quantities tend over time. Of course, the values taken by the state variables are decreasing functions of δ.

Before we introduce the simulations, we should note that the computer program is written so that the economy "ends" when capital is reduced to zero, which can occur in some experiments using a Leontief production function.

7.2 No R&D Activity

7.2.1 First COD-Simulation

For the Cobb–Douglas production function (from here on COD function) F, let us choose the values $\theta = 6$ and $\beta = 0.5$, i.e.

$$F(K_t, X_t) = 6K_t^{0.5}X_t^{0.5};$$

then (3.2) in Chapter 4, denoting firms' labour demand by N_t, becomes

$$N_t = 9\frac{K_t}{w_t^2}.$$

Of course, this is an increasing function of the stock of capital, and a decreasing function of the wage rate. For the parameter measuring the rate of decay of capital, let us choose the value $\delta = 0.2$. As already stated, with this choice of parameters there is a unique stationary state, given by the values

$$\hat{K} = 22500, \qquad \hat{w} = 45.$$

Finally, let us consider $\alpha = 0.1$, a low velocity parameter to clear the labour market and specify the starting values of capital and labour:

$$K_0 = 250, \qquad w_0 = 5.$$

The main result of the simulation, extended to the entire horizon of 120 time periods, is that, after a transitory phase of about 50 periods, roughly half the total time horizon, the economy is subjected only to very mild changes, of course converging to the stationary values, as shown by the time paths depicted in Figures COD1.1-2, where time is depicted on the horizontal axis while the captions denote which of the two state variables, capital, K_t, and wage rate, w_t, is shown.

Figure COD1.3 is the phase-space summarizing the preceding two figures, and shows very directly the convergence of the state variables to their stationary values.

Figure COD1.4 illustrates that the labour supply very quickly reaches its full employment value of 100 units, and that full employment is permanent. Labour demand, as depicted in Figure COD1.5, shows very strong oscillations up to period 35, and then reaches its permanent long run stationary value.

Figure 1.6 depicts the time behaviour of total production (GDP); after a wide oscillation, it permanently reaches the stationary value, i.e. $\hat{Y} = \theta F(\hat{K}, \hat{E}) = 6F(22500, 100) = 9000$.

Due to the fact that full employment is reached very quickly, and that the wage rate oscillates only up to period 50, total profits, too, display a time behaviour strongly resembling that of GDP. Figure COD1.8 depicts the per capita production which, as in the case of some of the previous variables, oscillates before reaching its stationary state value.

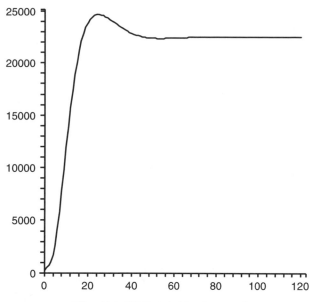

Fig. 7.1 COD 1.1: Total capital

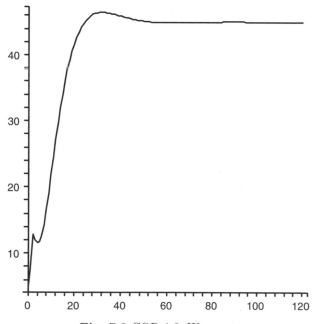

Fig. 7.2 COD 1.2: Wage rate

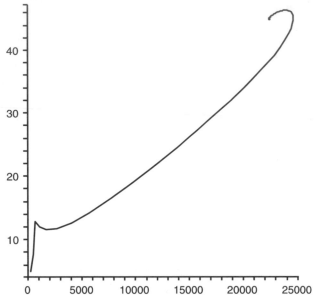

Fig. 7.3 COD 1.3: (K, w)-phase space

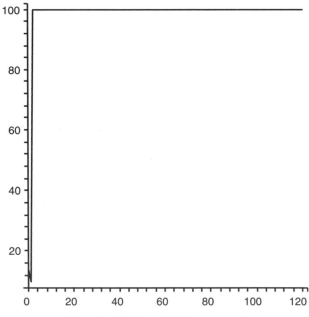

Fig. 7.4 COD 1.4: Labour supply

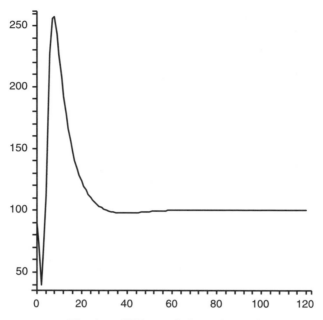

Fig. 7.5 COD 1.5: Labour demand

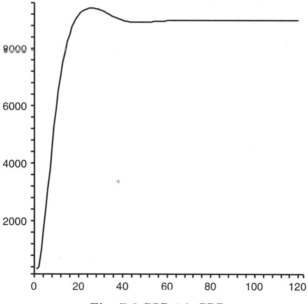

Fig. 7.6 COD 1.6: GDP

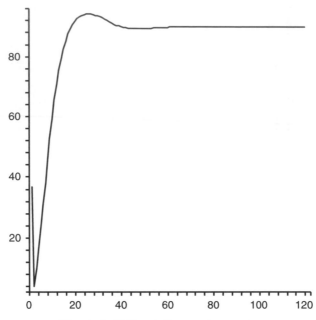

Fig. 7.7 COD 1.8: Pro capite product

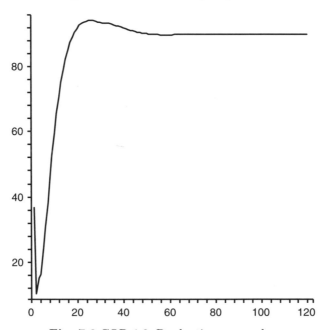

Fig. 7.8 COD 1.9: Production per worker

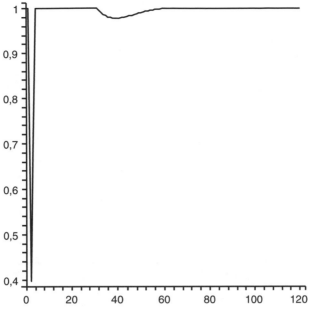

Fig. 7.9 COD 1.10: Employment ratio

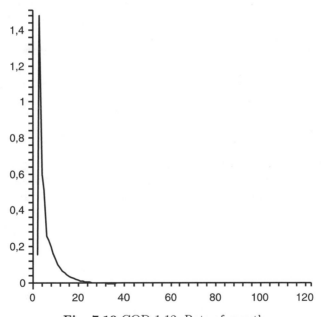

Fig. 7.10 COD 1.12: Rate of growth

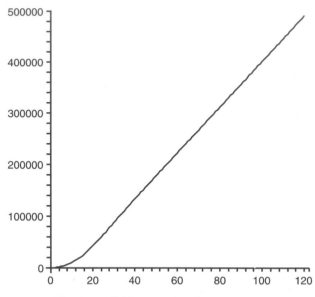

Fig. 7.11 COD 1.14: Total consumption

The time path is of course the same for production per worker, depicted in Figure 1.9, since the employment ratio, i.e. N_t/L_t, presented in Figure 1.10, quickly takes its full employment value, i.e. 1, but with a very small decrease in periods 31 to 60.

Since the fundamentals of the economy are stationary, the rate of growth, i.e. $\frac{Y_{t+1}-Y_t}{Y_t}$, which is depicted in Figure COD1.12, after a very extended transitory phase of about 25 periods fluctuates very mildly around zero.

From the last figure in this simulation, Figure COD1.14, we can see that total consumption increases steadily over time and the end amounts to $CT_{120} \approx 492000$.

It is interesting to increase the value of α, while keeping all other parameter values constant. It could be assumed that the only result of this increase would be a corresponding increase in the speed with which the stationary equilibrium values are approached, while the global time behaviour of the economy ought to be similar to the previous simulation, except in terms of the speed with which the values are achieved.

Despite this prima facie conclusion we find, and this is not limited only to the present simulation, by increasing α to quickly cover the discrepancy between labour demand and labour supply, the increase in α generates a transitory phase whose oscillations are very responsive to this variable, while at the same time reducing the number of periods before the economy starts to evolve regularly to its stationary values. But this is generally true only up to a certain point; when α approaches unity, oscillations in all variables become very severe over the entire time horizon, with no tendency to dampen.[1] Thus, it seems possible to state that it should be remembered, when designing economic policy interventions, that the influence of α could produce permanent effects on the economy. In other words, attempts to quickly remove the discrepancies between labour demand and supply could be very damaging to the economy and its evolution towards a stationary equilibrium.

Another point that arises strongly from many of the simulations,[2] is that very often increasing the adjustment velocity, α, every thing else being equal, introduces cycles in the variables of the model, which, in general, reduce total consumption in the economy, CT_{120}, which, as stated in the introduction to this part of the monograph, is considered to be a reliable index of material welfare.

7.2.2 Second COD-Simulation

By implementing this simulation, time paths are generated which look very different from those in the preceding simulation.

The following values for the parameters are selected:

$$\alpha = 0.2, \qquad \beta = 0.5, \qquad \delta = 0.2, \qquad \theta = 2;$$

in particular, the velocity chosen to close the discrepancy between labour demand and supply, α, is doubled with respect to the value chosen for the first simulation.

The same starting values chosen previously for the amount of capital and the wage rate are retained:

$$K_0 = 250, \qquad w_0 = 5.$$

The corresponding stationary values taken by the state variables are computed to be

$$\hat{K} = 350, \quad \hat{w} = 5;$$

thus, the starting wage rate equals its stationary value.

The main results of the simulation are shown in Figures COD2.1–14. It can be seen that the time paths of the main variables cycle around their stationary state values and, in particular, there are very mild and short irregular transitory phases when the wage rate reaches its peak values.

Every cycle lasts 36 periods, as shown by the state variables pictured in Figures COD2.1-2. The corresponding phase-space is plotted in Figure COD2.3.

All other variables manifest analogous time paths, as depicted in Figures COD2.4–12. Moreover, for some variables cycles are more irregular and pronounced than in the case of the wage rate.

---

[1] See the third COD simulation.
[2] See, e.g., the third COD simulation.

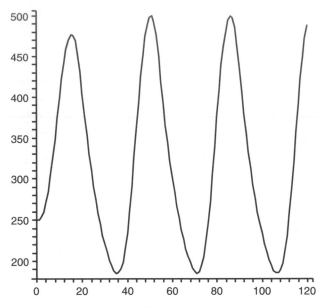

Fig. 7.12 COD 2.1: Total capital

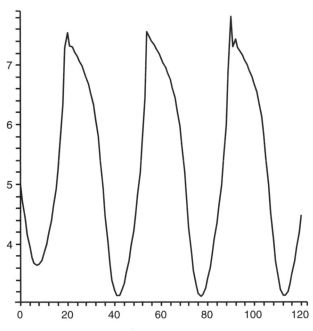

Fig. 7.13 COD 2.2: Wage rate

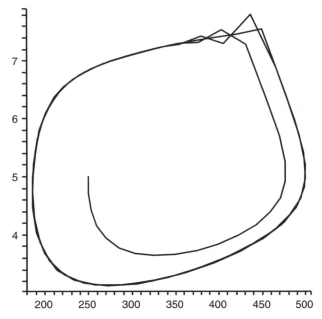

Fig. 7.14 COD 2.3: (K, w)-phase space

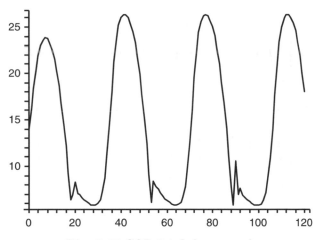

Fig. 7.15 COD 2.4: Labour supply

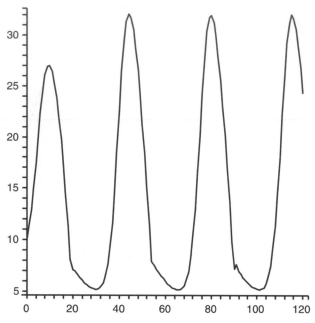

Fig. 7.16 COD 2.5: Labour demand

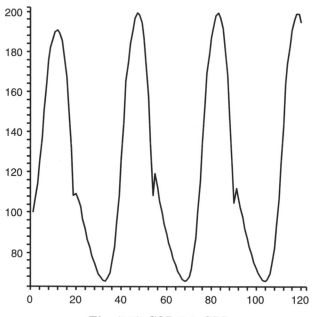

Fig. 7.17 COD 2.6: GDP

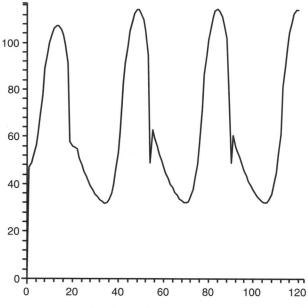

Fig. 7.18 COD 2.7: Profits

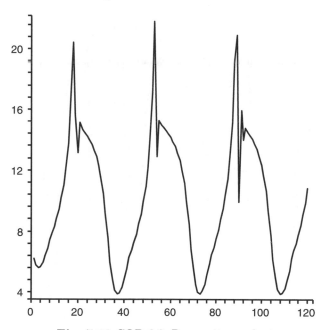

Fig. 7.19 COD 2.8: Pro capite product

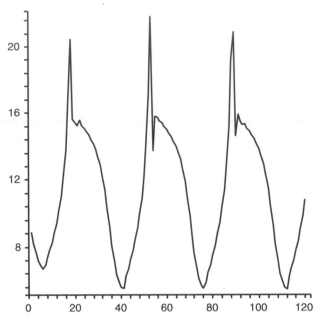

Fig. 7.20 COD 2.9: Production per worker

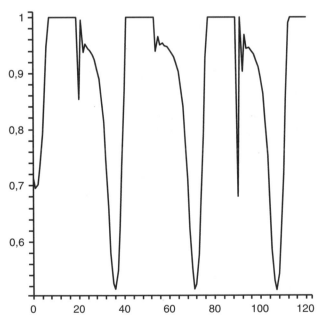

Fig. 7.21 COD 2.10: Employment ratio

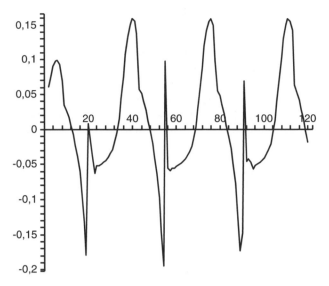

Fig. 7.22 COD 2.12: Rate of growth

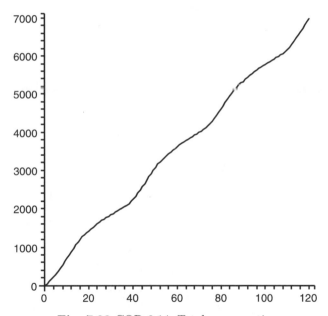

Fig. 7.23 COD 2.14: Total consumption

From Figure COD2.10, it is apparent that the employment ratio is frequently less than 1.

From Figure COD2.12 it appears that the relative rate of growth oscillates irregularly and widely across the entire time horizon.

Finally, total consumption grows steadily over the whole horizon, to the value $CT_{120} = 6960$; its final value is less than the same value obtained by the preceding simulation. This is due to the low value assigned to θ (here we have $\theta = 2$ while in the first simulation we had $\theta = 6$), and to the presence of cycles.

7.2.3 Third COD-Simulation

In this simulation the velocity parameter for adjusting the wage rate is increased to $\alpha = 0.5$. The other parameter values are $\theta = 6, \beta = 0.5, \delta = 0.6$, and the starting state variables are as in the preceding simulations:

$$K_0 = 250, \quad w_0 = 5.$$

As already stated in Section 1, the stationary values of the state variables are $\hat{K} = 2500$, $\hat{w} = 15$. Implementing the simulation shows very well that all variables vibrate continuously to the end of the horizon. The time series obtained for real economies frequently resemble those in Figures COD3.1-12 below, but of course with reduced amplitudes.

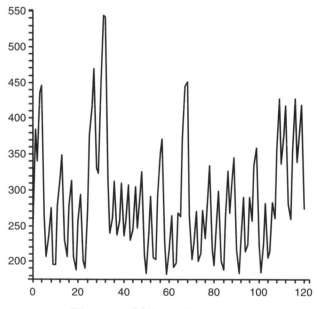

Fig. 7.24 COD 3.1: Total capital

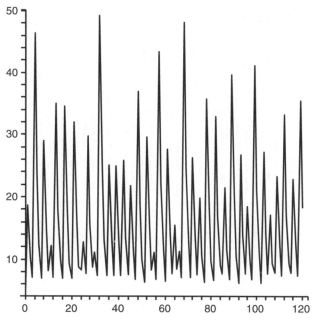

Fig. 7.25 COD 3.2: Wage rate

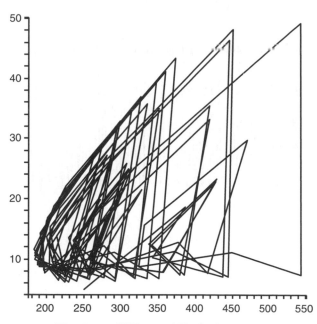

Fig. 7.26 COD 3.3: (K, w)-phase space

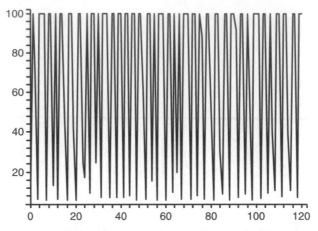

Fig. 7.27 COD 3.4: Labour supply

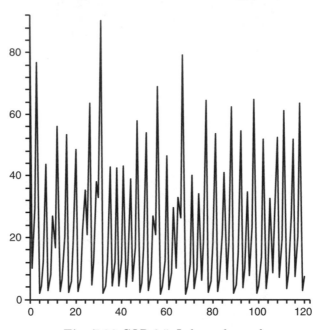

Fig. 7.28 COD 3.5: Labour demand

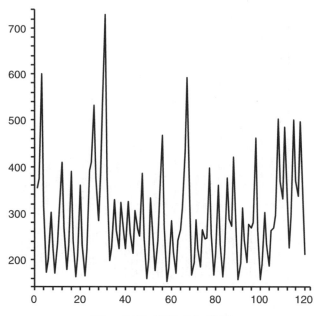

Fig. 7.29 COD 3.6: GDP

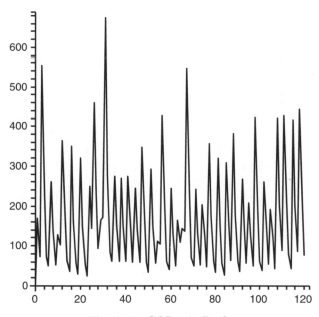

Fig. 7.30 COD 3.7: Profits

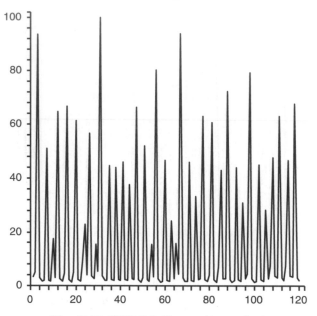

Fig. 7.31 COD 3.8: Pro capite product

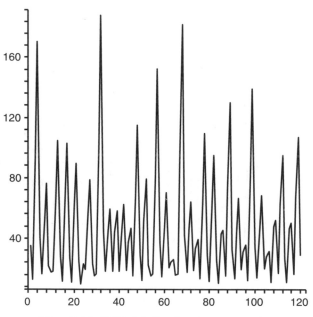

Fig. 7.32 COD 3.9: Production per worker

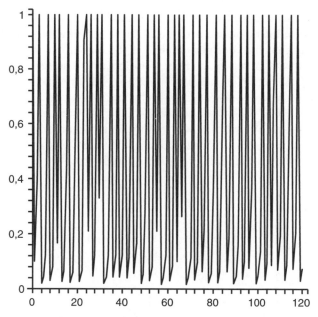

Fig. 7.33 COD 3.10: Employment ratio

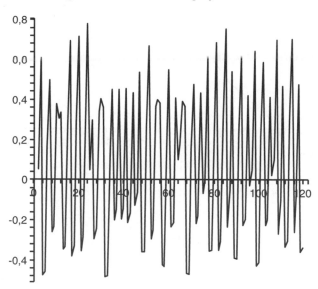

Fig. 7.34 COD 3.12: Rate of growth

It would seem reasonable to suppose that these time paths, which are mimicking deterministic chaos, are due to the high value of α, which imposes on the economy that in every period 50% of the labour excess demand should be considered to adjust the wage rate. Undoubtedly, the results of this simulation strongly support the choice of adjusting velocities very slowly, to help the system to converge to a stationary solution, when one is available.

Finally, we should note that, ceteris paribus, the economy performs much better when its variables vibrate only mildly. Indeed, total consumption along the whole time horizon for this simulation gives a low value for total consumption, $CT_{120} \approx 14000$, as revealed by Figure COD3.14.

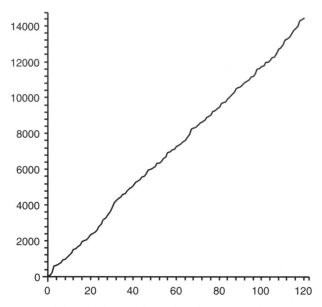

Fig. 7.35 COD 3.14: Total consumption

7.3 Positive R&D Expenditure

7.3.1 Fourth COD-Simulation

This subsection presents more simulations to show the powerful effect of expenditure on R&D, keeping labour supply stationary.

The parameters considered are the same as in the third simulation, i.e. $\alpha = 0.5$, $\beta = 0.5$, and $\delta = 0.6$, but with the addition of some new values:

$$\epsilon = 0.01, \quad c = 0.1, \quad d = 0.5,$$

for the fraction of profits devoted to R&D and for the parameters of the total productivity function respectively. 1% of total expenditure on investment devoted to R&D seems to be lower than the average values currently experienced in the so called first world economies. Moreover, we can set the starting values to be the same as in the third simulation, i.e.

$$K_0 = 250, \quad w_0 = 5, \quad \theta_0 = 6.$$

This simulation shows quite clearly that the erratic behaviour demonstrated in the third simulation is generally still present in the first 25 periods. After this, the strength of the R&D activity is such that the economy evolves steadily, as tested by Figures COD4.1–12. This behaviour can be explained, e.g., by the value of the total productivity parameter, presented in Figure 4.11; at the end of the horizon its value is $\theta_{120} = 16$, or just less than three times the starting value.

It is interesting once again to look at total consumption allowed by this simulation: from Figure 4.14 we obtain $CT_{120} \approx 543000$.

Comparing this value with the analogous value for the case of no R&D activity, i.e. $CT_{120} \approx 14000$ of the third COD simulation, the effectiveness, in the medium-long run, of investing even a small fraction of profits in R&D activity is quite clear.

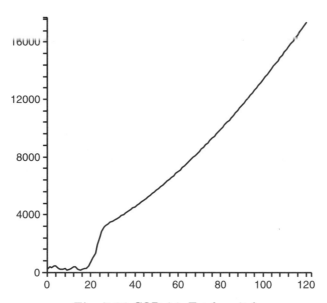

Fig. 7.36 COD 4.1: Total capital

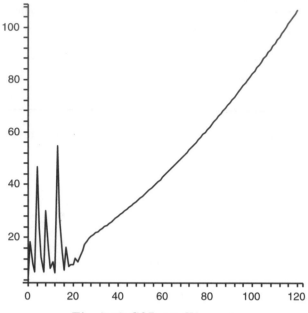

Fig. 7.37 COD 4.2: Wage rate

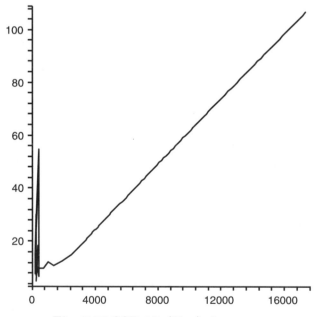

Fig. 7.38 COD 4.3: (K, w)-phase space

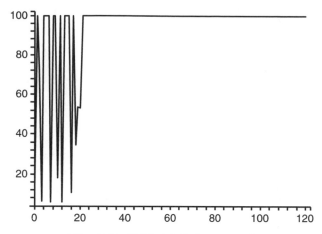

Fig. 7.39 COD 4.4: Labour supply

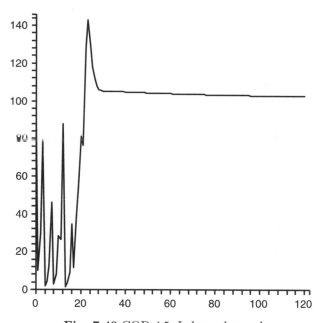

Fig. 7.40 COD 4.5: Labour demand

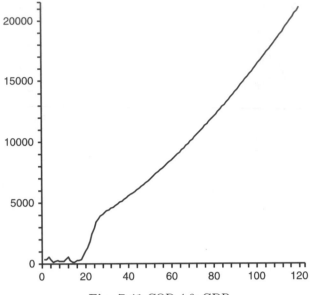

Fig. 7.41 COD 4.6: GDP

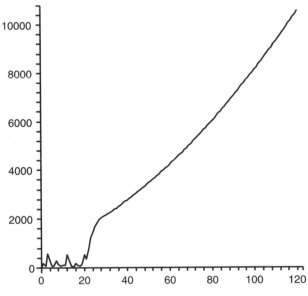

Fig. 7.42 COD 4.7: Profits

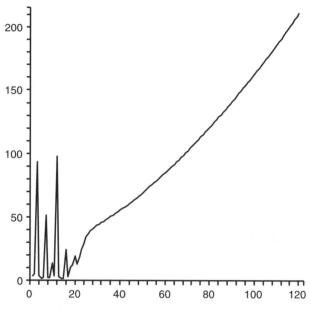

Fig. 7.43 COD 4.8: Pro capite product

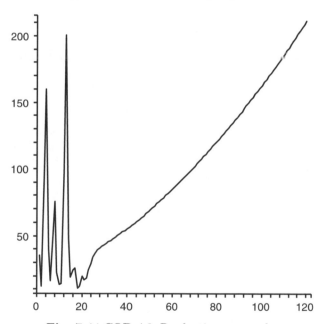

Fig. 7.44 COD 4.9: Production per worker

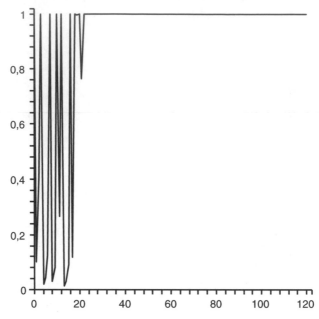

Fig. 7.45 COD 4.10: Employment ratio

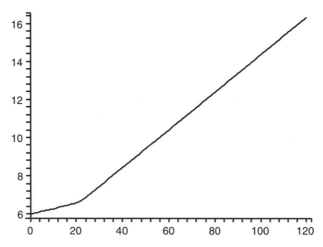

Fig. 7.46 COD 4.11: Productivity parameter

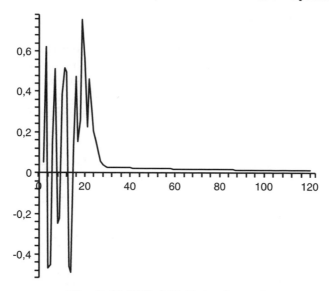

Fig. 7.47 COD 4.12: Rate of growth

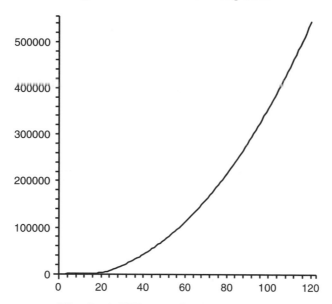

Fig. 7.48 COD 4.14: Total consumption

7.3.2 Fifth COD-Simulation

Let us now change only the value of the decay of capital parameter in the above simulation, and choose instead $\delta = 0.2$. The first result is that the transitory non-steady phase holds only for six periods, and after that the economy grows steadily, as shown by Figures COD5.1–14.

Note that the relative rate of growth, depicted in Figure COD5.12, after fluctuating for about 10 periods, decreases very slowly towards the value 0.012.

Finally, total consumption is $CT_{120} \approx 1.84 \times 10^6$, or more than four times the value when $\delta = 0.6$. In so far as the model in some sense mimics a real economy, the result obtained proves once more that the decay coefficient plays a very important role.

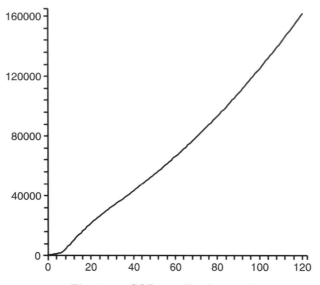

Fig. 7.49 COD 5.1: Total capital

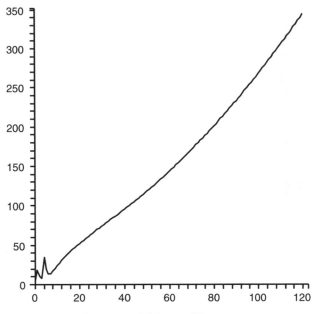

Fig. 7.50 COD 5.2: Wage rate

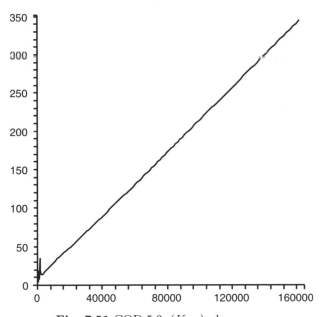

Fig. 7.51 COD 5.3: (K, w)-phase space

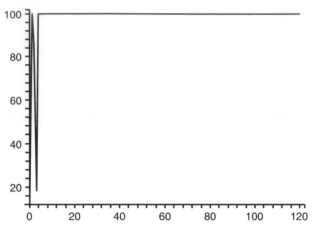

Fig. 7.52 COD 5.4: Labour supply

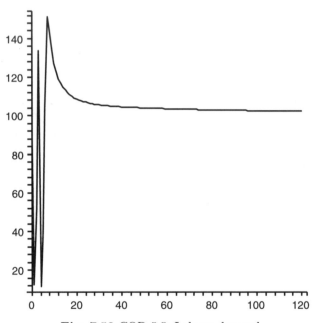

Fig. 7.53 COD 5.5: Labour demand

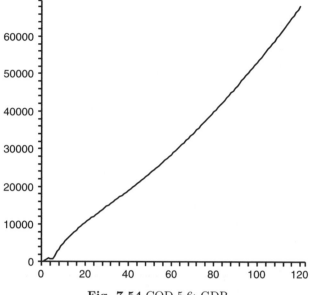

Fig. 7.54 COD 5.6: GDP

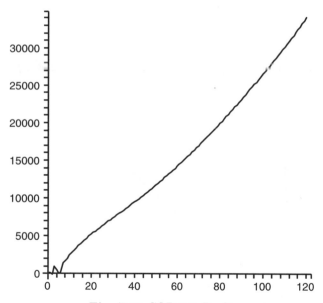

Fig. 7.55 COD 5.7: Profits

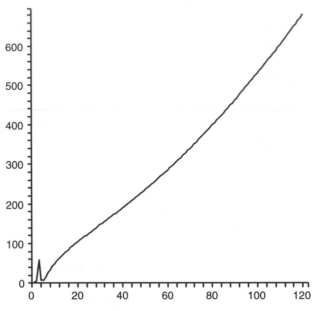

Fig. 7.56 COD 5.8: Pro capite product

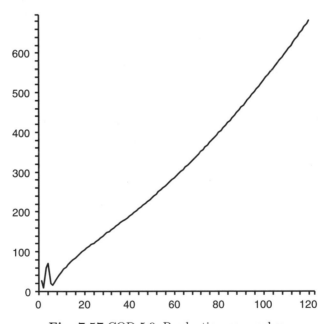

Fig. 7.57 COD 5.9: Production per worker

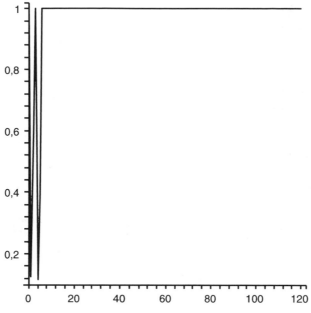

Fig. 7.58 COD 5.10: Employment ratio

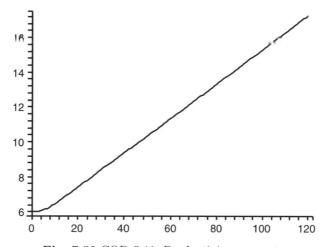

Fig. 7.59 COD 5.11: Productivity parameter

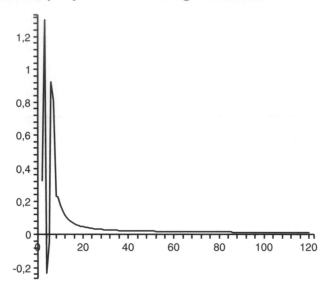

Fig. 7.60 COD 5.12: Rate of growth

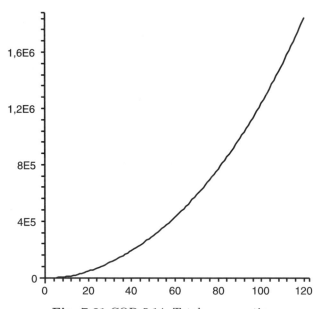

Fig. 7.61 COD 5.14: Total consumption

8

Stationary Population: CES Simulations

8.1 Introduction

Simulations with a CES production function show that they are extremely sensitive to the choice of parameters, especially the coefficients a and b in the production function. Simulations are also extremely sensitive to the choice of the value of β, given the same values for all other parameters, and given the same starting values for the state variables.

For the case of CES, under constant returns to scale, the production function is written

$$F(K_t, X_t) = \theta(aK_t^\beta + bX_t^\beta)^{1/\beta} \qquad\qquad (\beta \neq 0), \qquad\qquad (1.1)$$

where θ, a, and b are positive parameters;[1] the function expressing the optimal demand for labour looks as follows:

$$N_t = \frac{a^{1/\beta} K_t}{\left[\left(\frac{w_t}{b\theta}\right)^{\frac{\beta}{1-\beta}} - b\right]^{1/\beta}} \qquad\qquad (\beta \neq 0, \beta \neq 1). \qquad\qquad (1.2)$$

It is obvious, as was shown in Chapter 4, that the values of w_t, b, β, and θ must keep the denominator positive; thus, we have $w_t > \theta b^{1/\beta}$ when β is positive, while the inequality is reversed when β is negative. To implement the simulations, in the case that w_t becomes negative and assuming that w_{t-1} is positive, we will choose, according to convention, $w_t = w_{t-1}$. Moreover, N_t maximizes profits only when $\beta < 1$ is true, because only in this case is $\frac{\partial^2 \pi}{\partial X^2} < 0$, regardless of the sign of β.

---

[1] Of course, θ can be incorporated into the parameters a, b. But to assess the impact of the expenditure on R&D on the production function, it seems more useful to consider the parameter θ separately, because when implementing simulations under a positive R&D activity it is interesting to consider θ as a function of time, while keeping a and b constant.

The simulations presented keep all starting values for capital and wage rate constant, and also all parameters except β, which is selected in the open interval $(-\infty, 1)$. The common values for all CES simulations are

$$\alpha = 0.02, \delta = 0.5, a = 0.5, b = 1$$

for the parameters, and the starting values for the state variables are $K_0 = 10$, $w_0 = 2$. Moreover, for every simulation with a positive β we can write $\theta = 1$; for simulations implemented when β is negative we have $\theta = 10$. The latter is due to the fact that when β is negative only small values of the wage rate ensure positivity of the optimal labour demand function (see Chapter 4).

8.2 No R&D Activity

8.2.1 First CES-Simulation

Let us choose $\beta = 0.5$. The simulation shows that there are two cycles in the state variables, depicted in Figures CES1.1–3, in which cycles are strongly damped.

The cycle depicted in Figure CES1.3 shows very clearly the convergence to stationary values, i.e. $\hat{K} = 104.96$ and $\hat{w} = 2$. Labour demand and supply also are subject to two damped cycles, shown in Figures CES1.4-5: GDP displays similar behaviour, according to Figure CES1.6.

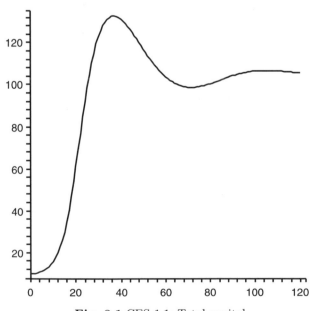

Fig. 8.1 CES 1.1: Total capital

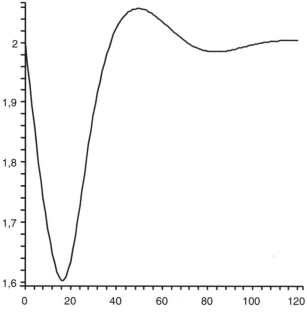

Fig. 8.2 CES 1.2: Wage rate

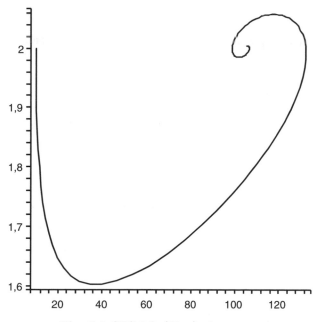

Fig. 8.3 CES 1.3: (K, w)-phase space

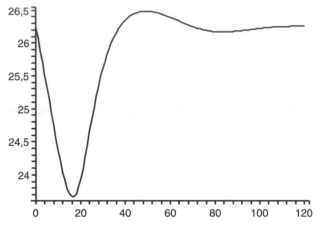

Fig. 8.4 CES 1.4: Labour supply

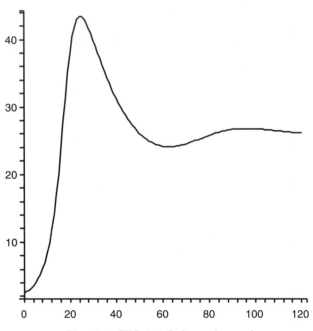

Fig. 8.5 CES 1.5: Labour demand

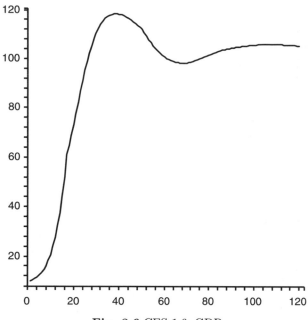

Fig. 8.6 CES 1.6: GDP

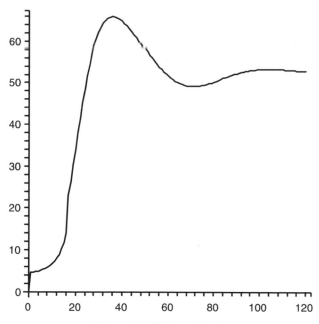

Fig. 8.7 CES 1.7: Profits

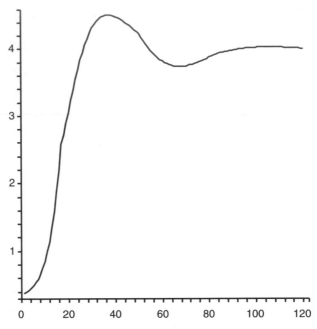

Fig. 8.8 CES 1.8: Pro capite product

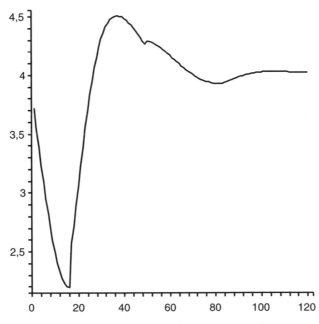

Fig. 8.9 CES 1.9: Production per worker

Other variables too undergo the same type of time behaviour, as tested by the next three figures:

Figure CES1.10 is of interest in terms of the employment ratio, which increases rapidly in the first 16 periods, from 0.11 to 1, indicating full employment. After that, it remains at the full employment value for most of the time, apart from a slight decrease during the time interval between periods 49 and 84.

The rate of growth fluctuates irregularly, as depicted in Figure CES1.12, and from period 100 on it is more or less equal to zero.

Finally, in this simulation, total consumption amounts to $CT_{120} = 5430$.

This value should be compared with the analogous value obtained when, starting from the stationary values $\hat{K} = 104.96$ and $\hat{w} = 2$, the economy generates total consumption of $CT_{120} = 6290$. As in other situations described in Chapter 7, here too total consumption in the stationary state is significantly greater than when the economy fluctuates, starting from a non-stationary state.

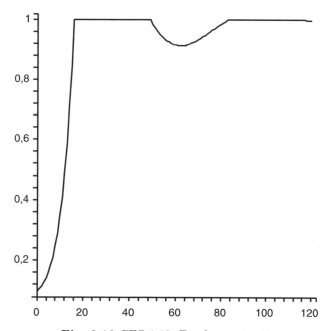

Fig. 8.10 CES 1.10: Employment ratio

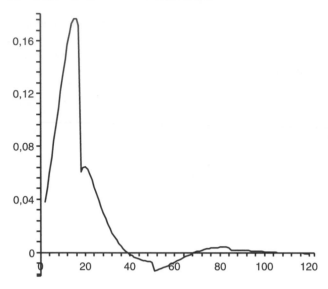

Fig. 8.11 CES 1.12: Rate of growth

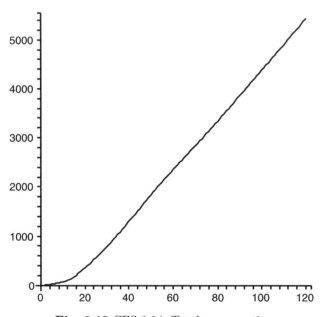

Fig. 8.12 CES 1.14: Total consumption

8.2.2 Second CES-Simulation

Let us choose the same values as in the first simulation, except to make $\beta = 0.2$. Correspondingly, the stationary values of the state variables are $\hat{K} = 3200$, and $\hat{w} = 16$. The simulation shows, according to Figures CES2.1–14, that the economy cycles around the stationary values,[2] with a transitory short phase of four periods, when some variables change very slightly.

After that, the economy experiences two cycles around the stationary values, the second not fully completed because the number of periods is maintained at $n = 120$. Rate of growth shows some differences to this time behaviour; in the first 20 periods it fluctuates slightly, before oscillating around zero.

Total consumption amounts to $CT_{120} \approx 167600$. Comparing this value to that in the previous simulation, i.e. $CT_{120} = 5430$, we see that changing only the parameter β has a very heavy impact on the material welfare of the economy.

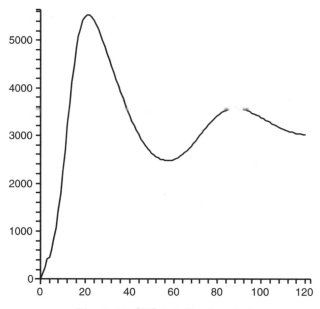

Fig. 8.13 CES 2.1: Total capital

---

[2] Except for production per worker presented in Figure CES2.9.

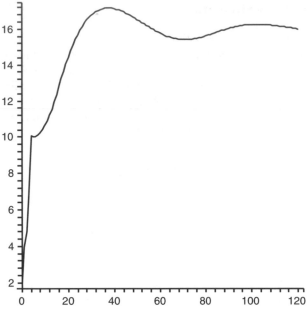

Fig. 8.14 CES 2.2: Wage rate

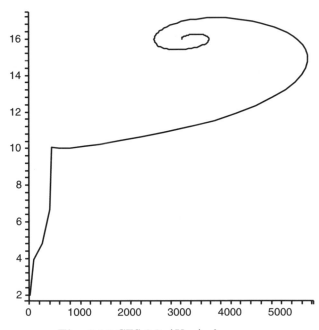

Fig. 8.15 CES 2.3: (K, w)-phase space

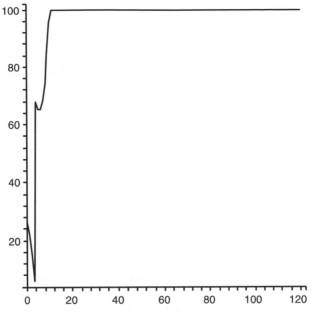

Fig. 8.16 CES 2.4: Labour supply

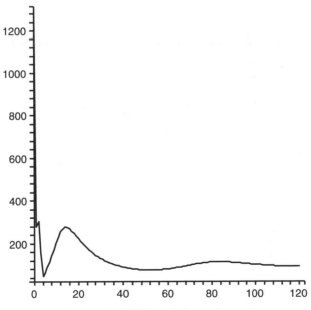

Fig. 8.17 CES 2.5: Labour demand

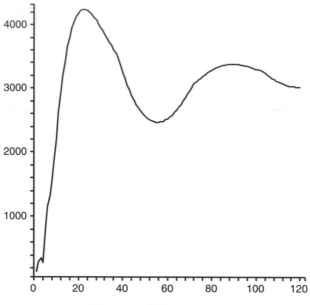

Fig. 8.18 CES 2.6: GDP

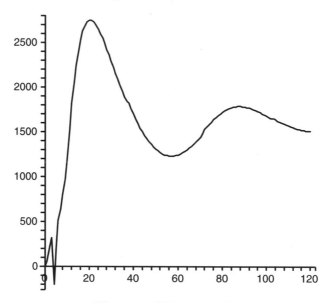

Fig. 8.19 CES 2.7: Profits

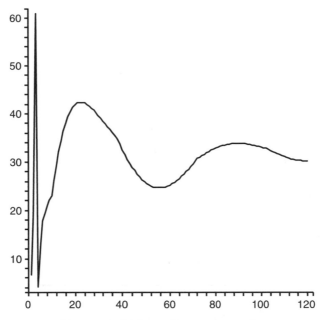

Fig. 8.20 CES 2.8: Pro capite product

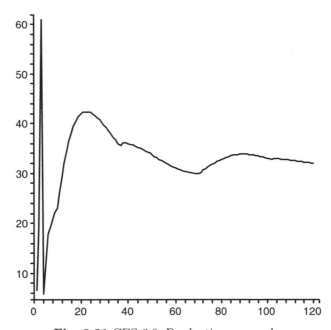

Fig. 8.21 CES 2.9: Production per worker

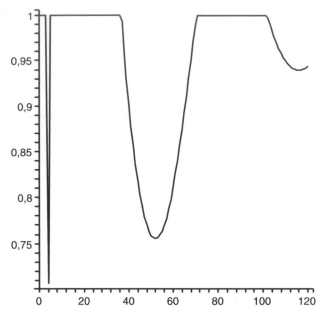

Fig. 8.22 CES 2.10: Employment ratio

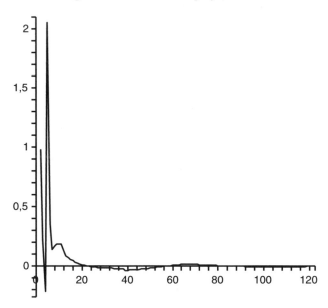

Fig. 8.23 CES 2.12: Rate of growth

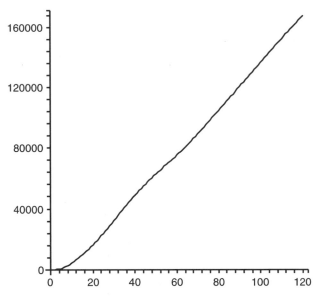

Fig. 8.24 CES 2.14: Total consumption

8.2.3 Third CES-Simulation

Let us now examine what happens if the values $\theta = 10$ and $\beta = -0.2$ are chosen. The results are summarized in Figures CES3.1–14.

A curious characteristic of this numerical experiment is that capital begins to decrease rapidly towards a very small value of the order of magnitude of 10^{-6}, reached in period 45. The value of capital stays extremely low up to period 76, when it starts increasing, to attain its maximum value in period 94, i.e. $K_{94} = 18.3$. After that time, capital again decreases attaining the value $K_{120} = 9.4$, which is a bit less than the starting capital, $K_0 = 10$. In terms of the wage rate, this decreases steadily up to period 82, reducing in value from 2 to 0.4, and then increasing up to 0.855 in period 107, to then decrease again towards the value $w_{120} = 0.825$.

Labour supply and labour demand show quite different time paths; while, as can be seen from Figure CES3.4, supply decreases steadily to period 80, demand for labour shown in Figure CES3.5 decreases very rapidly in the first four periods to a value of almost zero, which is maintained to period 76, when it increases sharply, to reach 35 in period 88, decreasing once more to 10.93 in period 118. In the last two periods labour demand increases again.

The employment ratio, depicted in Figure CES3.10, while close to zero in the first 75 periods, increases sharply to 1 (i.e. full employment) in period 80, which is maintained to period 106; after that, it decreases to 0.8, to increase again in the last three periods of the horizon.

The rate of growth, from Figure CES3.12, is subject to a very wide oscillation, starting from -0.4 to reach a peak of about 1.4, in period 80. Afterwards

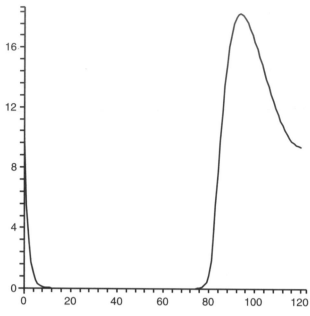

Fig. 8.25 CES 3.1: Total capital

this rate rapidly decreases to zero and then oscillates mildly up to the end of the time horizon.

Finally, as depicted in Figure CES3.13, consumption becomes truly positive only from period 75; it increases steeply up to period 107 and then decreases gradually.

Total consumption begins increasing significantly only from period 80 on, and reaches the value $CT_{120} = 352$.

It goes without saying that this simulation does not represent any real situation; the behaviour of the time series up to period 70 is that of an economy suffering major starvation, as occurred frequently in the Middle Ages, and in the present day occurs in some African regions, where local wars cause major decrease in their populations and GDP.

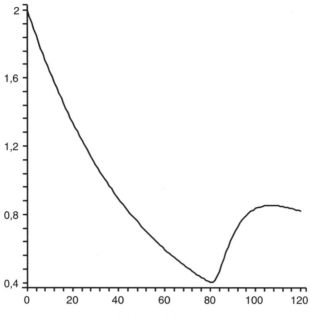

Fig. 8.26 CES 3.2: Wage rate

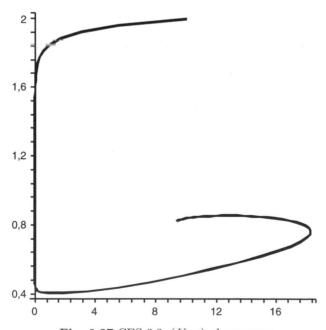

Fig. 8.27 CES 3.3: (K, w)-phase space

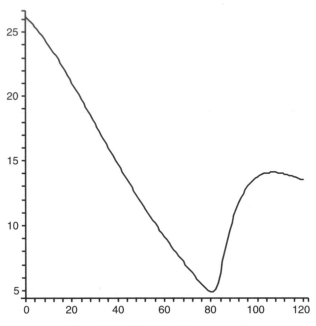

Fig. 8.28 CES 3.4: Labour supply

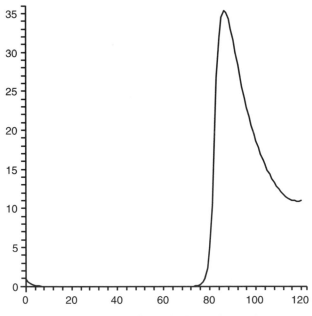

Fig. 8.29 CES 3.5: Labour demand

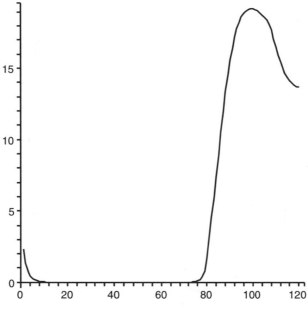

Fig. 8.30 CES 3.6: GDP

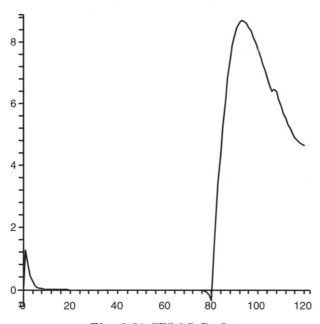

Fig. 8.31 CES 3.7: Profits

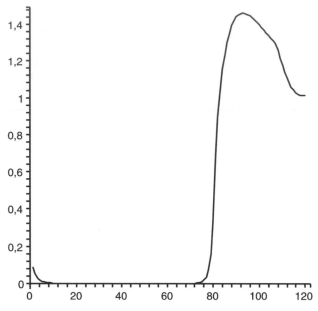

Fig. 8.32 CES 3.8: Pro capite product

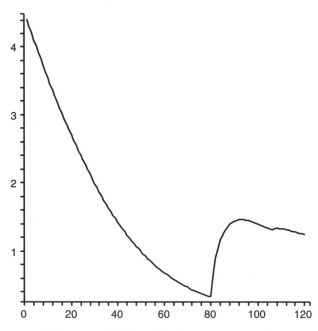

Fig. 8.33 CES 3.9: Production per worker

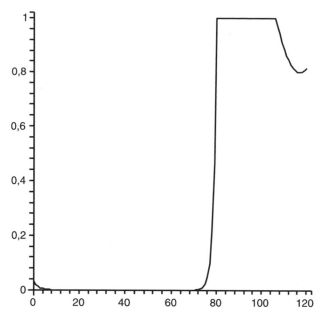

Fig. 8.34 CES 3.10: Employment ratio

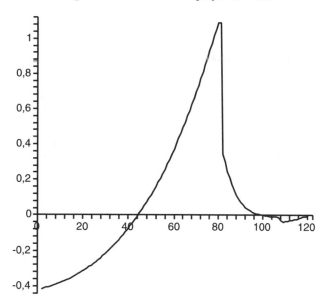

Fig. 8.35 CES 3.12: Rate of growth

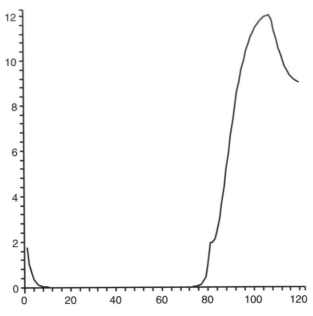

Fig. 8.36 CES 3.13: Consumption

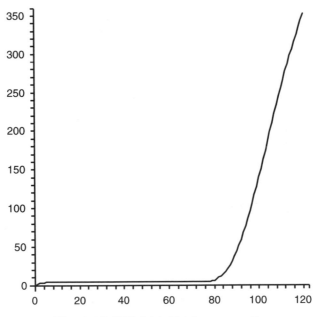

Fig. 8.37 CES 3.14: Total consumption

8.2.4 Fourth CES-Simulation

This simulation is implemented for the value $\beta = -0.5$, while all other parameters and the starting values are as in the preceding simulation. The results of this exercise are depicted in Figures CES4.1–14.

The state variables, as the corresponding set of figures shows (namely Figures CES4.1–3), undergo four cycles,[3] whose amplitudes decrease with time.

Of course, cycles occur around the stationary values of the state variables, i.e. $\hat{K} = 50$ and $\hat{w} = 4.5$, as Figure CES4.3 quite clearly proves. Cycles for capital, wage rates, labour supply and demand, and GDP, are quite regular (see Figures CES4.4–6):

Figures CES4.7 and CES 4.9 show that profits and production per worker oscillate rather irregularly.

The employment ratio, whose time path is presented in Figure CES4.10, also cycles, and frequently reaches the full employment value, while its lowest values, i.e. the minimum values taken by this ratio, are increasing over time. The rate of growth too, as graphically presented in Figure CES4.12, oscillates somewhat irregularly and, of course, oscillations are damped around the stationary value zero. Lastly, it can be seen in Figure CES4.13 that consumption oscillates, and total consumption, whose time path is presented in Figure CES4.14, attains the value $CT_{120} = 7850$.

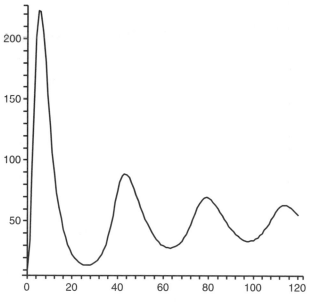

Fig. 8.38 CES 4.1: Total capital

---

[3] The fourth cycle is not completed, because the time horizon is arrested at 120 time periods.

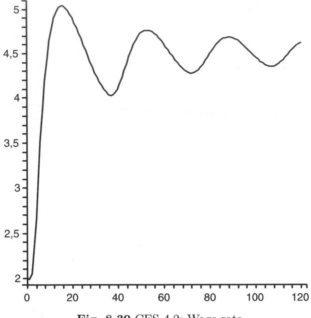

Fig. 8.39 CES 4.2: Wage rate

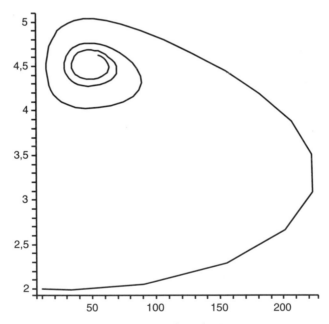

Fig. 8.40 CES 4.3: (K, w)-phase space

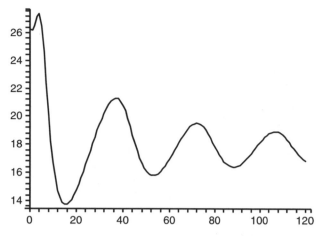

Fig. 8.41 CES 4.4: Labour supply

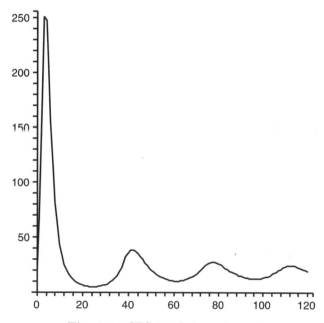

Fig. 8.42 CES 4.5: Labour demand

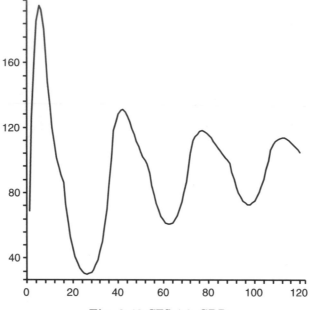

Fig. 8.43 CES 4.6: GDP

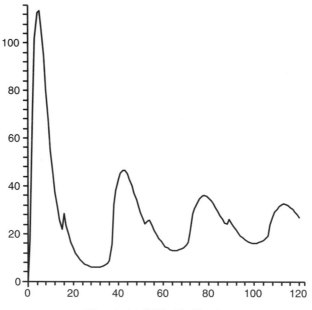

Fig. 8.44 CES 4.7: Profits

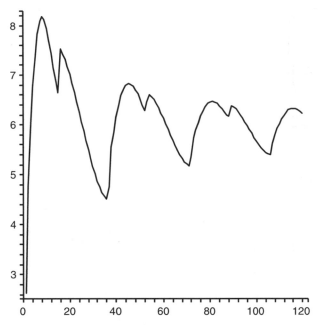

Fig. 8.45 CES 4.9: Production per worker

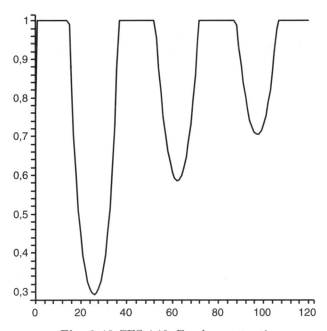

Fig. 8.46 CES 4.10: Employment ratio

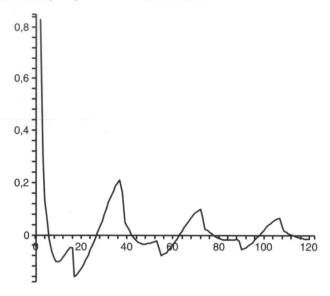

Fig. 8.47 CES 4.12: Rate of growth

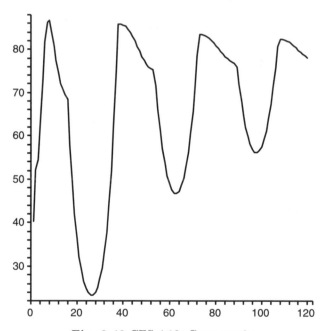

Fig. 8.48 CES 4.13: Consumption

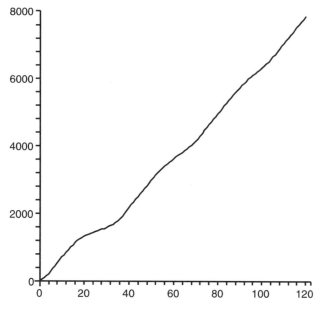

Fig. 8.49 CES 4.14: Total consumption

8.3 Positive R&D Expenditure

Let us now consider the CES-economy when a positive expenditure on R&D is introduced. The positive parameter ϵ, measuring the percentage of profits invested in R&D, in every period is $\epsilon = 0.01$, while the coefficients of the R&D production function are $c = 0.1$ and $d = 0.5$. As noted elsewhere, $\epsilon = 0.01$ is a low value, since advanced economies invest about 3% of their GDP in R&D activity.

8.3.1 Fifth CES-Simulation

Using the common parameters and starting values as in the previous simulation, and considering $\theta_0 = 10$, we obtain Figures CES5.1–14. In Figure CES5.11, the productivity parameter, θ_t, increases steadily from its starting value, $\theta_0 = 10$, to its final value, $\theta_{120} = 61.1$; i.e., productivity grows more than sixfold by the end of the chosen horizon.

From Figure CES5.1, it can be seen that total capital oscillates with an increasing trend in the first 64 periods, and then grows steadily. The wage rate, however, shown in Figure CES5.2, is subject only to a mild oscillation in the first periods, before increasing steadily. A possible explanation for these differences is that in the starting periods profits devoted to R&D, ceteris paribus, decrease the quota devoted to investment, which increases labour productivity and wage rate. From Figure CES5.4, we can see that labour supply cycles upward to period 45, adopting a permanent maximum value of 100, while labour demand, depicted in Figure CES5.5, shows two wide oscillations, before decreasing steadily up to the end of the horizon when its value is still greater than the full employment value.

GDP, after two mild oscillations in the first periods, grows steadily, since after these initial periods productivity growth becomes very effective:

Profits become negative in period 10, as can be seen from Figure 5.7, after which time, and after two minor oscillations, they are positive and steadily increasing up to the end of the horizon. The employment ratio, depicted in Figure CES5.10, is generally equal to 1, except for an oscillation with a bottom value of 0.77, between periods 12 and 21. Finally, rate of growth, depicted in Figure CES5.12, after reaching economically unreasonable values from the first period up to period 12, becomes slightly negative, then definitely positive from period 18 on; it reaches a new peak of about 17% in period 45 and then it decreases up to the end of the horizon.

The fact that the economy can grow, based on expenditure on R&D, makes it difficult to explain the behaviour of the rate of growth. Perhaps one explanation for its behaviour is the high wage rate due to labour shortage, shown in Figure CES5.5. Lastly, total consumption amounts to $CT_{120} = 208000$, and grows steadily from period 20 on.

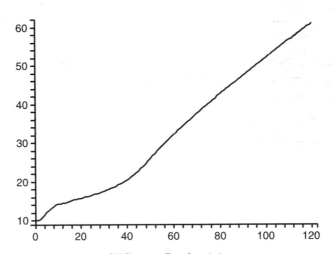

Fig. 8.50 CES 5.11: Productivity parameter

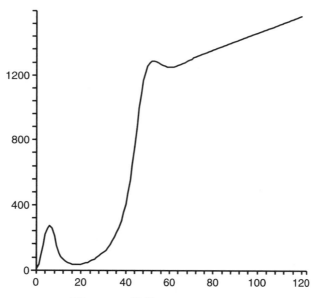

Fig. 8.51 CES 5.1: Total capital

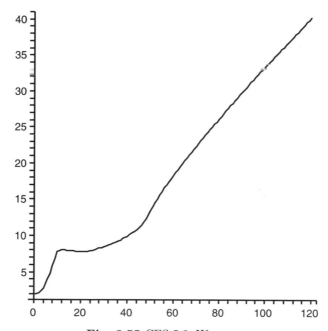

Fig. 8.52 CES 5.2: Wage rate

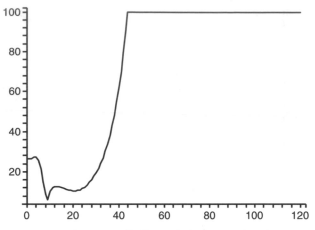

Fig. 8.53 CES 5.4: Labour supply

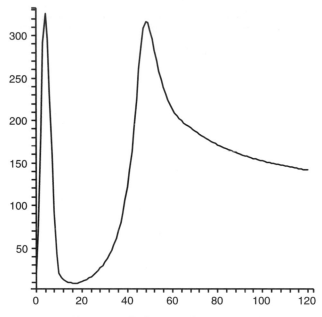

Fig. 8.54 CES 5.5: Labour demand

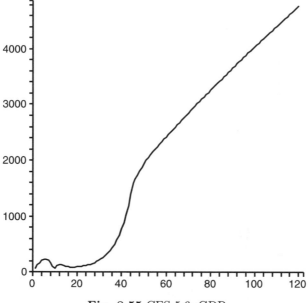

Fig. 8.55 CES 5.6: GDP

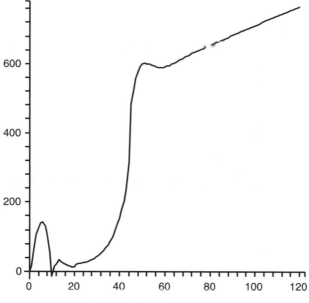

Fig. 8.56 CES 5.7: Profits

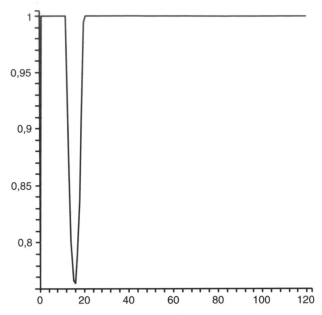

Fig. 8.57 CES 5.10: Employment ratio

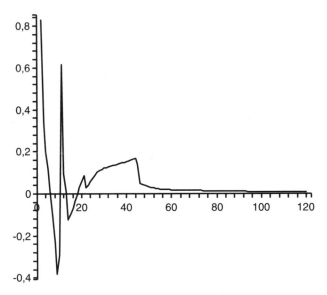

Fig. 8.58 CES 5.12: Rate of growth

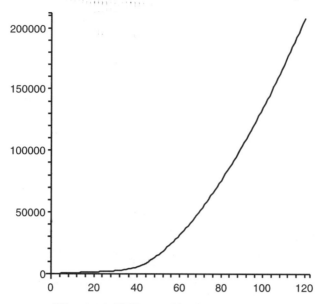

Fig. 8.59 CES 5.14: Total consumption

8.3.2 Sixth CES-Simulation

We conclude this simulation section by considering the starting values of the state variables $K_0 = 10$, $w_0 = 2$, $\theta_0 = 10$, and the parameter value $\epsilon = 0.001$, keeping everything else as in the previous simulation. The expenditure from profits is reduced compared to the fifth simulation. The results of this simulation are contained in Figures CES6.1–14. In terms of the behaviour of the state variables, we can see that they undergo three cycles; while capital does not begin to increase until period 70, the wage rate shows increasing oscillations from the start of the time horizon.

Labour supply and demand also show cycles; the supply of labour, in particular, is always very low, compared to the maximum potential supply. This, of course, is due to the fact that the wage rate is too low to motivate workers to supply more labour time. But labour demand is also very low, in spite of wage rates being low.

Figure CES6.6 shows that GDP cycles for the first 62 periods, before starting an accelerating growth path. Profits and per capita production (Figures CES6.7 and 6.8) also show a cyclic behaviour before growing steadily towards the end of the time horizon. Production per worker (Figure CES6.9) shows a similar time path, but with more complex cycles, while employment ratio (Figure CES6.10) has two extremely low values.

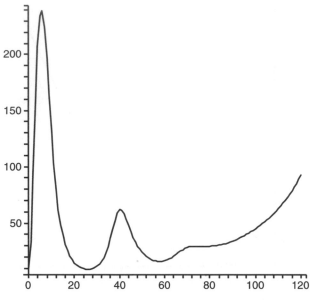

Fig. 8.60 CES 6.1: Total capital

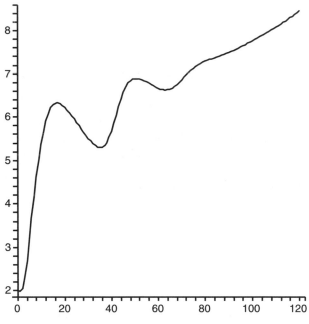

Fig. 8.61 CES 6.2: Wage rate

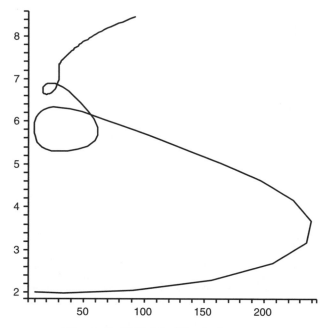

Fig. 8.62 CES 6.3: (K, w)-phase space

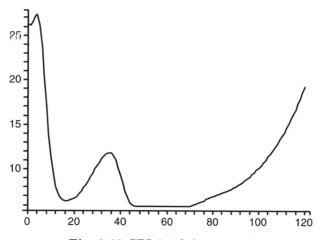

Fig. 8.63 CES 6.4: Labour supply

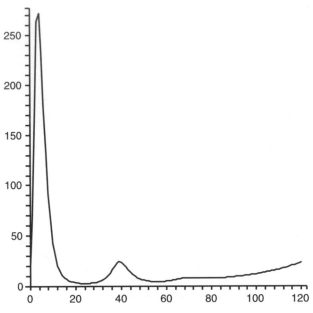

Fig. 8.64 CES 6.5: Labour demand

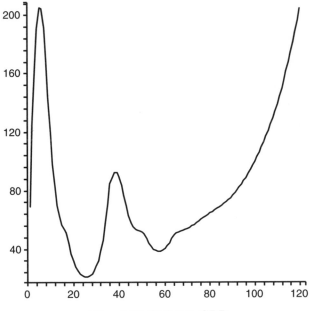

Fig. 8.65 CES 6.6: GDP

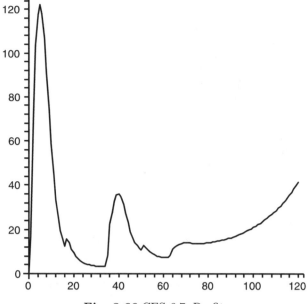

Fig. 8.66 CES 6.7: Profits

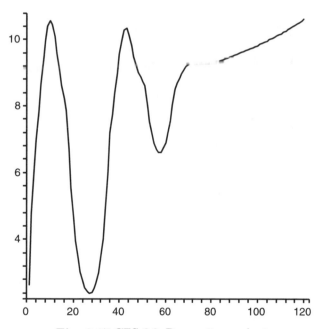

Fig. 8.67 CES 6.8: Pro capite product

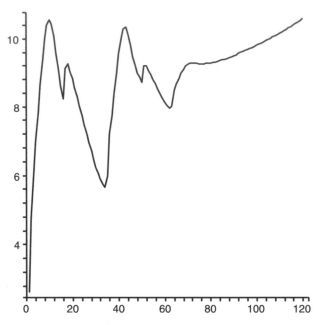

Fig. 8.68 CES 6.9: Production per worker

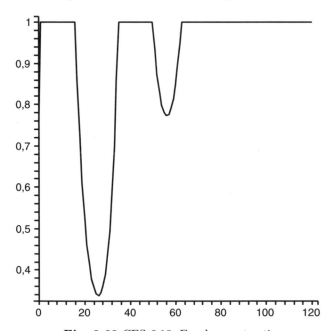

Fig. 8.69 CES 6.10: Employment ratio

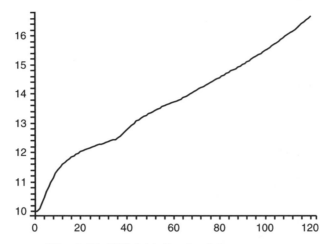

Fig. 8.70 CES 6.11: Productivity parameter

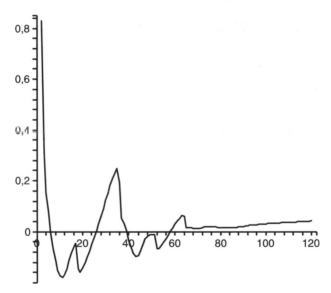

Fig. 8.71 CES 6.12: Rate of growth

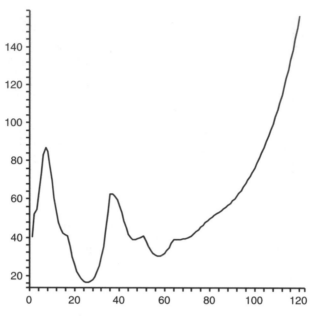

Fig. 8.72 CES 6.13: Consumption

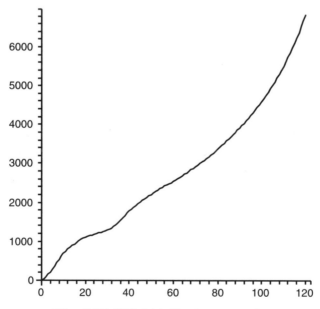

Fig. 8.73 CES 6.14: Total consumption

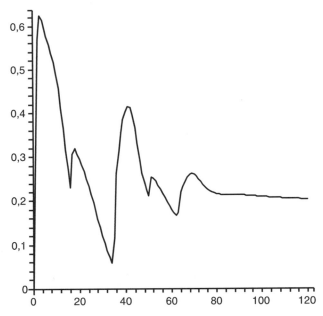

Fig. 8.74 CES 6.15: Percentage of profits in GDP

The productivity parameter, θ_t, depicted in Figure 6.11, increases only slowly, to reach the value $\theta_{100} = 17$; this may be explained by the extremely low value chosen for ϵ, which limits the impact of R&D expenditure.

Rate of growth, after some slight and rather chaotic oscillations around zero in the first half of the time horizon, becomes permanently positive.

Lastly, after fluctuating in the first 75 periods, consumption increases steadily at an increasing rate, as shown in Figure CES6.13.

Total consumption reaches a value $CT_{120} = 6840$ at the end of the horizon, which is a much smaller value than in the fifth simulation, proving once more that R&D expenditure can be very beneficial in terms of material welfare.

To conclude, the percentage of profits in GDP, plotted in Figure CES6.16, oscillates between values of 1.66% and 62% up to period 80, and thereafter remains fairly constant at around 21%. Of course, these values must be considered too variable to be realistic, especially when compared to the analogous values obtained in the COD simulations.

8.4 Afterthought

The richness of the time paths obtained in the CES simulations is, in one sense, rather suspect, especially when compared to the COD production function simulations in Chapter 7. Is it a virtue of the flexibility of CES functions or a serious shortcoming?

9

Stationary Population: Leontief Simulations

9.1 Introduction

This case corresponds to the following production function:

$$F(K_t, X_t) = \theta \min\{aK_t, bX_t\}, \tag{1.1}$$

for θ, a, b positive parameters. Given the amount of capital, K_t, according to Section 3 of Chapter 4 this production function generates the following demand function for labour:

$$N_t = \frac{a}{b} K_t \qquad (\theta b > w_t); \tag{1.2}$$

otherwise we have

$$N_t = 0 \qquad (\theta b \leq w_t). \tag{1.3}$$

Indeed, since output has been chosen as a numeraire, θb measures the marginal productivity of labour input.

Today Leontief production functions are of only historical interest; the numerous simulations that can be implemented with them, only some of which are reported here, show that the time paths generated for the various economic quantities are extremely sensitive to the choice of parameters, especially the productivity parameters, a and b, and the wage adjusting velocity, α.

9.2 No R&D Activity

9.2.1 First LEO-Simulation

The following parameter values are chosen:

$$\theta = 2, \quad a = 0.5, \quad b = 10, \quad \delta = 0.2, \quad \alpha = 0.1;$$

the stationary state corresponding to these parameters is:

$$\hat{K} = 2000, \quad \hat{w} = 16.$$

Finally, the starting values chosen for the state variables are:

$$K_0 = 120, \quad w_0 = 8.$$

Based on these values, the results of the simulation are depicted in Figures LEO1.1–14. Figures LEO1.1–2 show that, after a short transitory phase of about 10 periods, the state variables, K_t and w_t, are subject to smooth cycles, lasting for about 24 periods each, which decrease in size and converge to the stationary values.

In the phase space (K_t, w_t), depicted in Figure LEO1.3, these converging cycles are illustrated very clearly.

In terms of labour, it is interesting that while supply rapidly and permanently reaches its ceiling value, demand is subject to damped cycles. This behaviour can be explained by the permanently high wage rate along every cycle, which induces workers to supply the whole quantity of disposable labour all the time.

The time path for GDP, depicted in Figure LEO1.6, can be seen to oscillate with regularity, but with decreasing amplitude over time, and with five flat tracts due to the fact that labour supply is upper constrained by the value 100.

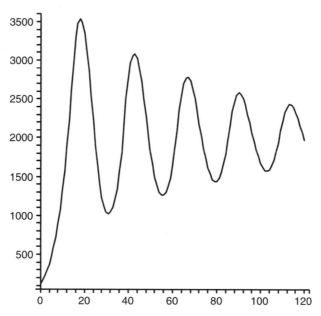

Fig. 9.1 LEO 1.1: Total capital

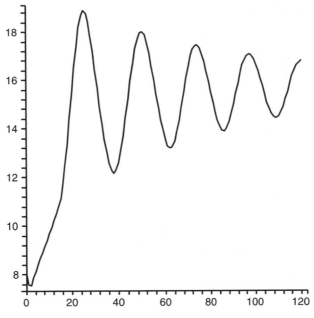

Fig. 9.2 LEO 1.2: Wage rate

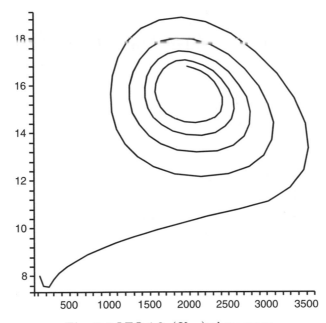

Fig. 9.3 LEO 1.3: (K, w)-phase space

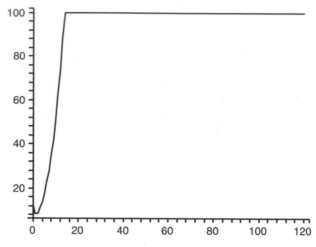

Fig. 9.4 LEO 1.4: Labour supply

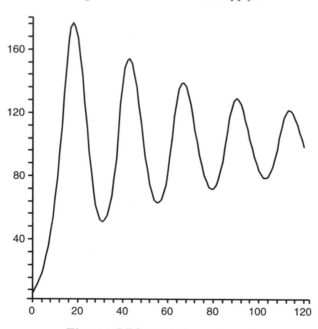

Fig. 9.5 LEO 1.5: Labour demand

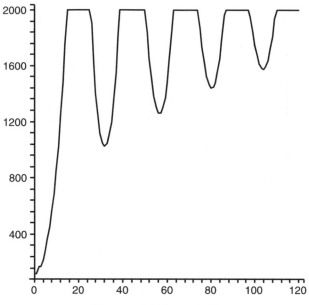

Fig. 9.6 LEO 1.6: GDP

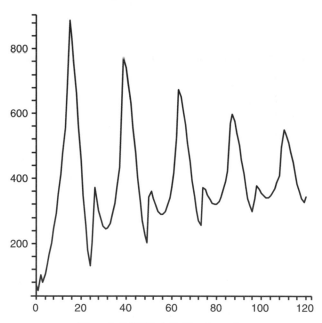

Fig. 9.7 LEO 1.7: Total profits

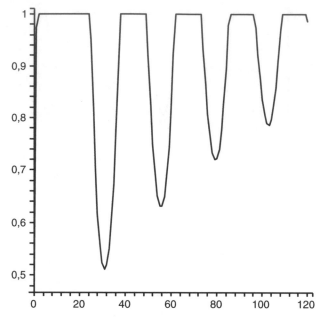

Fig. 9.8 LEO 1.10: Employment ratio

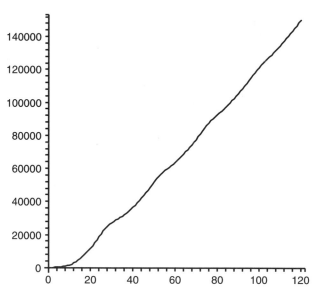

Fig. 9.9 LEO 1.14: Total consumption

Other variables, e.g. profits, are subject to cycles that are not at all smooth, as shown in Figure LEO1.7. Of course, all cycling variables display an average stationary-like behaviour, due to the fact that the model is tailored to stationary parameters. From Figure LEO1.10: we can see that, after a very short transitory, the employment ratio oscillates, frequently hitting its maximum value 1, while the minimum values increase over time.

Total consumption is $CT_{120} \approx 150000$, while in the stationary state, for starting values $K_0 = 2000$ and $w_0 = 16$, equal to the corresponding stationary values, we obtain $CT_{120} = 192000$, or a total consumption about 28% greater than the total consumption when, ceteris paribus, the economy is subject to cycles. Once more, we see that cycles per se do not favour growth.

9.2.2 Second LEO-Simulation

To implement this simulation we have chosen an adjustment velocity $\alpha = 0.2$, keeping all other parameter values and starting state variables constant.

Figures LEO2.1–2 show that now the number of cycles is increased but that oscillations are still regular, and occur around the same values as in the first LEO simulation. It should be noted that, as depicted in Figure LEO2.3, after an initial period all cycles move around almost the same values; thus, the stationary values of the state variables do not attract trajectories.

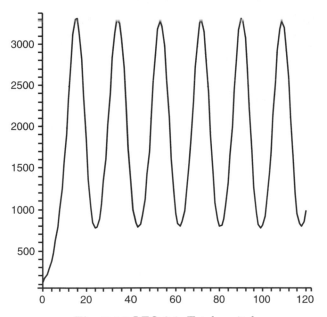

Fig. 9.10 LEO 2.1: Total capital

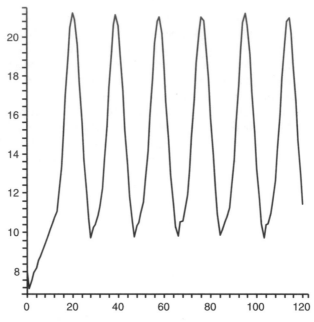

Fig. 9.11 LEO 2.2: Wage rate

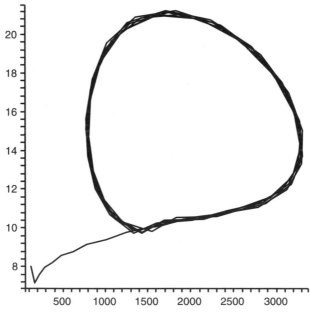

Fig. 9.12 LEO 2.3: (K, w)-phase space

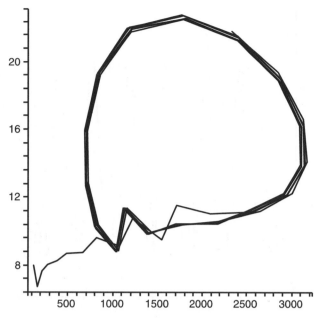

Fig. 9.13 LEO 2.3a: (K, w)-phase space

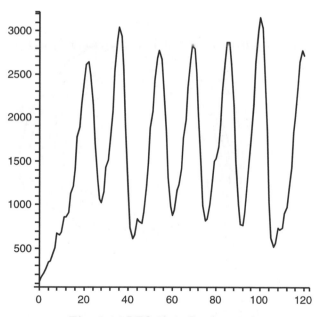

Fig. 9.14 LEO 2b.1: Total capital

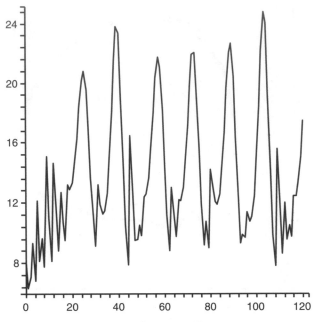

Fig. 9.15 LEO 2b.2: Wage rate

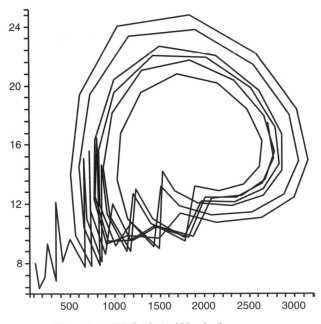

Fig. 9.16 LEO 2b.3: (K, w)-phase space

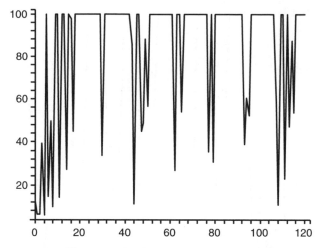

Fig. 9.17 LEO 2b.4: Labour supply

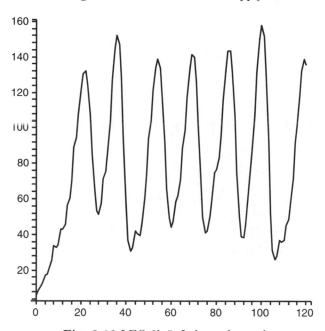

Fig. 9.18 LEO 2b.5: Labour demand

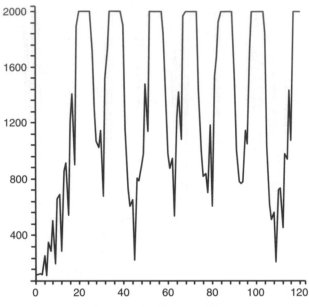

Fig. 9.19 LEO 2b.6: GDP

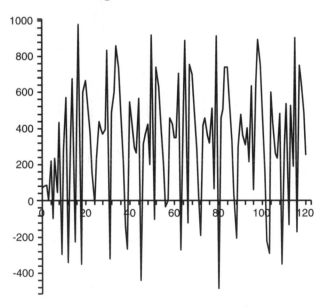

Fig. 9.20 LEO 2b.7: Total profits

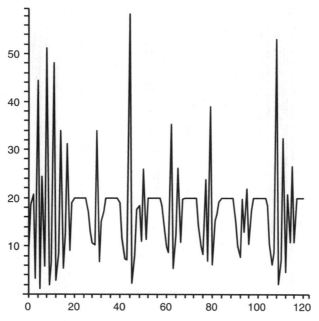

Fig. 9.21 LEO 2b.8: Pro capite product

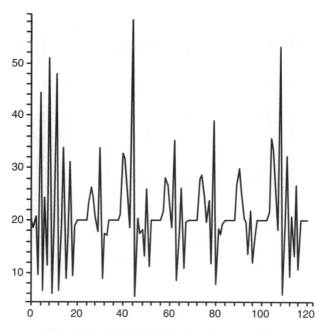

Fig. 9.22 LEO 2b.9: Production per worker

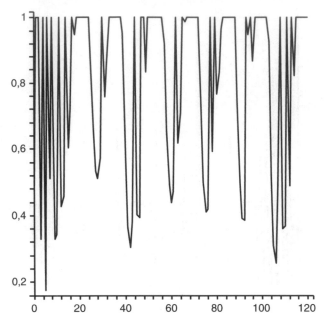

Fig. 9.23 LEO 2b.10: Employment ratio

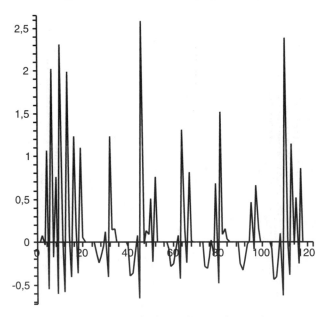

Fig. 9.24 LEO 2b.12: Rate of growth

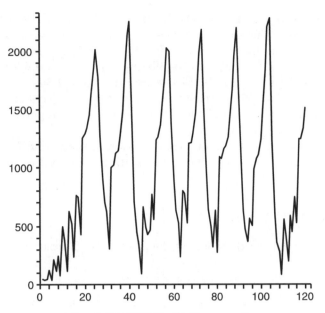

Fig. 9.25 LEO 2b.13: Consumption

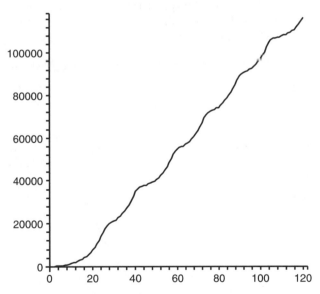

Fig. 9.26 LEO 2b.14: Total consumption

For comparison purposes, total consumption is $CT_{120} = 127900$, less than the corresponding value of the previous simulation, due to the fact that the cycles are shorter and more numerous. Further increasing the velocity to $\alpha = 0.3$, shows quite clearly that, while oscillating, the main variables are subject to irregular cycles, which can be clearly seen in Figure 2.3a:

Increasing the adjusting velocity to $\alpha = 0.4$, the economy behaves in a rather chaotic-like way, clearly depicted in many of the Figures LEO2b.1–14 and requires no further comment.

Note that in Figure 2b.14, total consumption amounts to $CT_{120} \approx 116000$, which, as expected, is less than the corresponding values in the previous simulations.

9.2.3 Third LEO-Simulation

Let us now change the values only of the production function coefficients. Let us put
$$a = 2, \quad b = 10,$$

with all other parameters and starting values the same as in the first LEO simulation.

The trajectories of the economic quantities look very different from those in the first LEO simulation. The wage rate, depicted in Figure LEO3.2, increases to the extent of absorbing the whole of the product of the economy, and capital

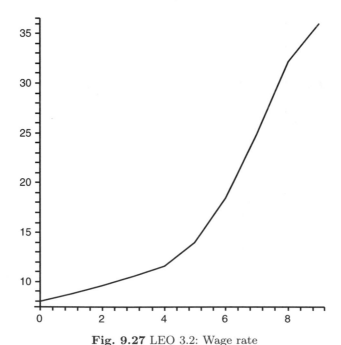

Fig. 9.27 LEO 3.2: Wage rate

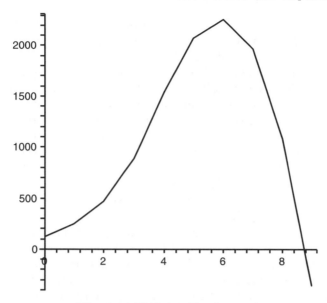

Fig. 9.28 LEO 3.1: Total capital

(see Figure LEO3.1) in period nine becomes negative, so that the economy reaches its domesday!

The marked differences between the CES and Cobb Douglas simulations and these simulations are due to the fact that with only one technique at the disposal of the economy, there is no possibility of obtaining any degree of substitution between the two inputs of labour and capital; with a Cobb–Douglas production function or a CES production function, on the other hand, substitution is always possible. This reinforces the consideration that the Leontief technology provides a very poor representation of the working of a modern economy, at both theoretical and applied macroeconomic levels.

9.3 Positive R&D Expenditure

In the case of Cobb–Douglas, the production function, F, is multiplied by the productivity parameter giving

$$F(K_t, X_t) = \theta_t \min\{aK_t, bX_t\}. \tag{3.1}$$

Because θ_t multiplies both productivity coefficients, a and b, optimal labour demand is still expressed by function (1.2) or function (1.3).

9.3.1 Fourth LEO-Simulation

Here, all starting data are the same as in the first LEO simulation; the value $\epsilon = 0.01$ is chosen to denote the percentage of profits devoted to R&D activity, with the values $c = 0.1$ and $d = 0.5$ representing the R&D production function, as in the fourth COD simulation in Chapter 7. The results obtained are summarized in Figures LEO4.1–14.

The time behaviour of the state variables is depicted in Figures LEO4.1–2. Somewhat surprisingly, expenditure on R&D, instead of generating a permanent and positive effect on the evolution of the economy, produces cycles, and reduces the capital endowment to zero after only 46 time periods.

In between, both state variables undergo two wide cycles, and the first minimum value of K_t remains close to zero. In period 46 the wage rate is $w_{46} = 63$; it is so high as to render the economy infeasible. The state space, corresponding to the preceding two figures, is as follows:

The next series of figures depicts the time series of some of the other variables. Note the marked differences in the time paths of labour supply and demand; of course, they are mainly due to the upper bound on labour supply and to the high wage rate. In Figures LEO4.8–9, the difference in time paths is very wide, while in the COD simulations these time paths were quite similar.

The employment ratio shows a decrease around period 28, and the productivity parameter doubles over time. However, this is not enough to balance out the huge increase in the wage rate:

The rate of growth, shown in Figure LEO4.12, oscillates between totally unrealistic values, confirming once more that the Leontief method is a poor tool for an analysis of the dynamic behaviour of an economy. Consumption in

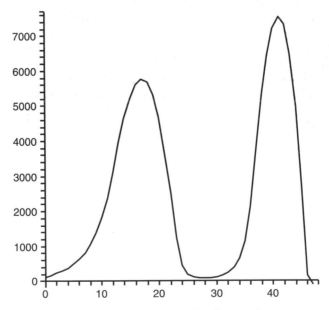

Fig. 9.29 LEO 4.1: Total capital

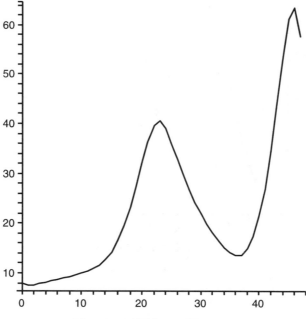

Fig. 9.30 LEO 4.2: Wage rate

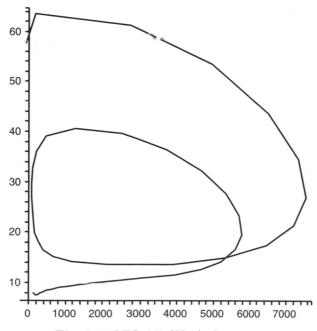

Fig. 9.31 LEO 4.3: (K, w)-phase space

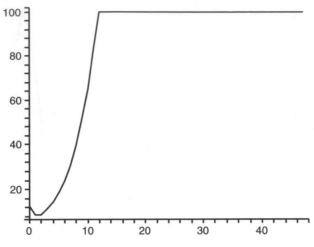

Fig. 9.32 LEO 4.4: Labour supply

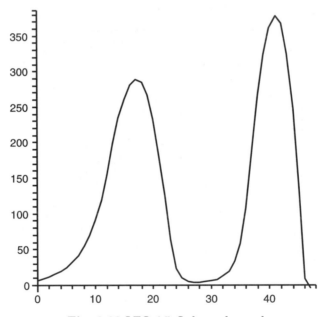

Fig. 9.33 LEO 4.5: Labour demand

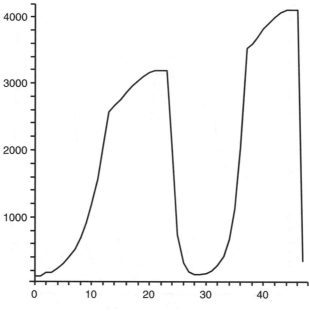

Fig. 9.34 LEO 4.6: GDP

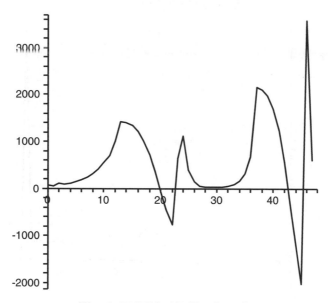

Fig. 9.35 LEO 4.7: Total profits

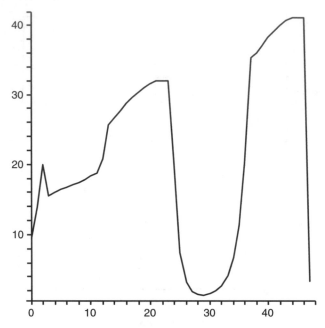

Fig. 9.36 LEO 4.8: Pro capite product

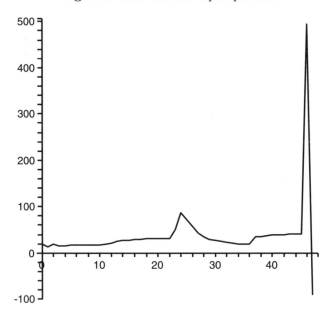

Fig. 9.37 LEO 4.9: Production per worker

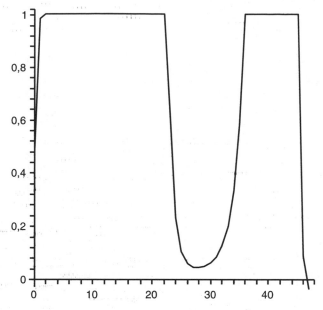

Fig. 9.38 LEO 4.10: Employment ratio

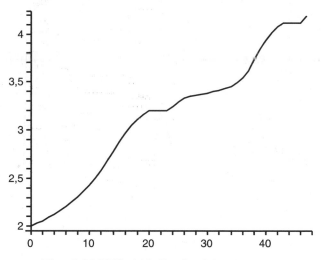

Fig. 9.39 LEO 4.11: Productivity parameter

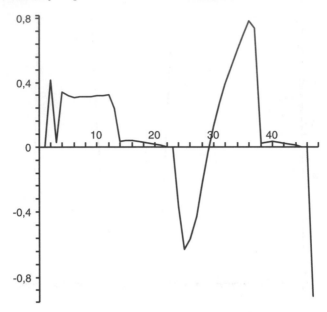

Fig. 9.40 LEO 4.12: Rate of growth

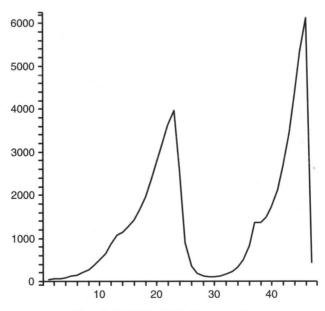

Fig. 9.41 LEO 4.13: Consumption

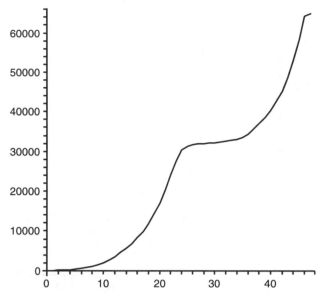

Fig. 9.42 LEO 4.14: Total consumption

every period, and total consumption, are presented in Figures LEO4.13 and 4.14, which gives us $CT_{47} = 64000$.

9.3.2 Fifth LEO-Simulation

The last in this set of simulations considers all the values employed in the preceding simulation except the velocity of adjustment of the wage rate, which is now reduced to $\alpha = 0.02$. This means that the wage rate changes very slightly from period to period. Figures LEO5.1–14 summarize the time behaviour of the main variables; note that the economy is viable along the entire time horizon.

Considering the time paths of the state variables and their state space, depicted in Figures LEO5.1–3, we can see that there are three cycles in the chosen horizon but, while for capital cycles are damped and seemingly stationary, wage rate cycles are damped, but subject to an increasing trend. It is probable that along a much longer horizon, the wage rate would become so high as to absorb the whole GDP, thereby ending the simulated economy.

As in the preceding experiment, supply and demand for labour have distinct time series: Again, an explanation for this marked difference is that there is a ceiling on labour supply, while demand responds only to an optimization criterion; thus, only labour demand is subject to cycles.

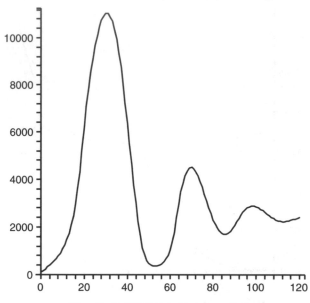

Fig. 9.43 LEO 5.1: Total capital

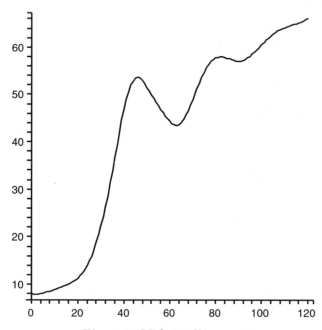

Fig. 9.44 LEO 5.2: Wage rate

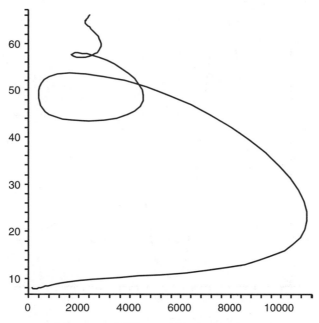

Fig. 9.45 LEO 5.3: (K, w)-phase space

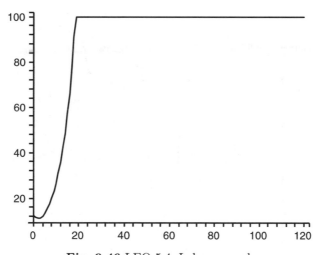

Fig. 9.46 LEO 5.4: Labour supply

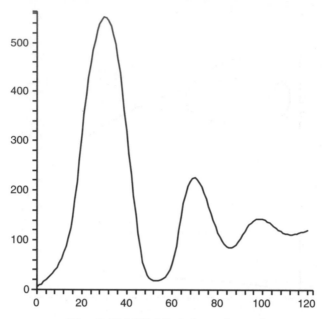

Fig. 9.47 LEO 5.5: Labour demand

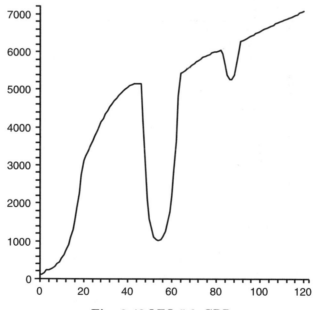

Fig. 9.48 LEO 5.6: GDP

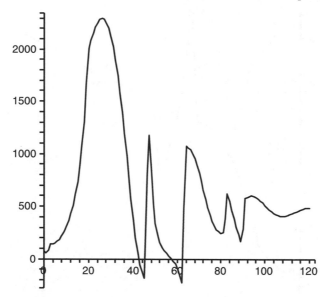

Fig. 9.49 LEO 5.7: Total profits

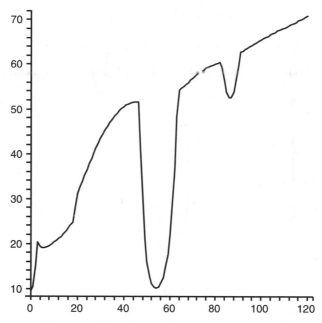

Fig. 9.50 LEO 5.8: Pro capite product

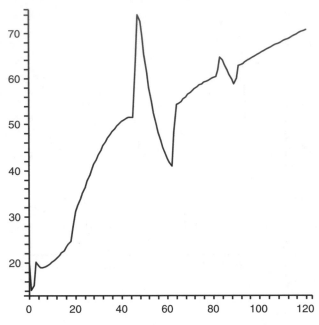

Fig. 9.51 LEO 5.9: Production per worker

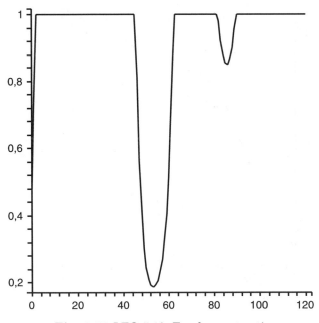

Fig. 9.52 LEO 5.10: Employment ratio

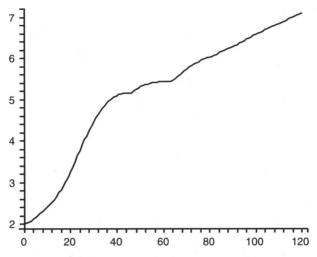

Fig. 9.53 LEO 5.11: Productivity parameter

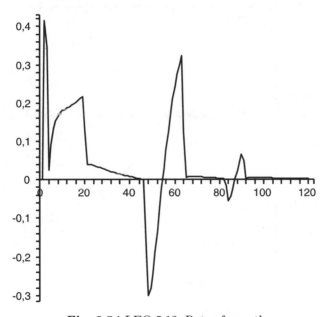

Fig. 9.54 LEO 5.12: Rate of growth

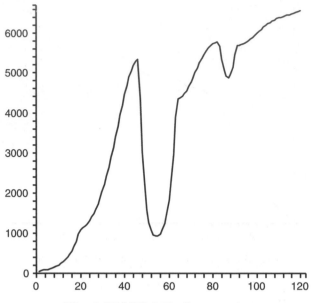

Fig. 9.55 LEO 5.13: Consumption

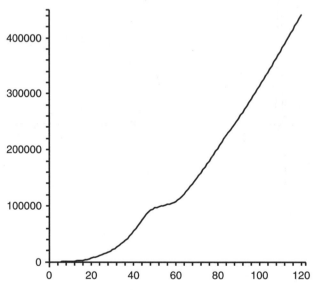

Fig. 9.56 LEO 5.14: Total consumption

The next figure, relating to GDP, illustrates the fact that production is subject to cycles with an increasing trend. Profits, on the other hand, oscillate irregularly and continuously, and at two points in time they become negative: Per capita production shows time behaviour similar to that for GDP, depicted in Figure LEO5.8. The correlation between GDP and per capita production is remarkable. The bottom values in Figures 5.6 and 5.8 are the same in the next two time series:

From Figure LEO5.11, we can see that the productivity parameter, θ_t, grows from a starting value of $\theta_0 = 2$ to value $\theta_{120} = 7.12$, a meaningful increase, bearing in mind that in every period only 1 percentage point of profits is devoted to R&D activity.

Figure LEO5.12 shows that the rate of growth twice becomes negative, corresponding to the bottom peaks in Figures LEO5.9–10. There are no discernible trends in this figure: it is as if there were no expenditure on R&D, which reconfirms the poor approximation, provided by the Leontief simulations, of the production sphere in present day economies.

Consumption demonstrates the same low peaks previously observed, while total consumption at the end of the horizon is $CT_{120} \approx 440000$: This value is significantly greater than the values reported at the end of the first LEO simulation. Thus, again it can be stated that in the medium-long run R&D counts a lot, at least in terms of increased per capita consumption.

10

Steady Growing Population

10.1 Introduction

Some of the simulations presented in the previous chapters are repeated here
in relation to population, and thus labour supply, which are increasing on time
according to a steady rate. We restrict this to Cobb–Douglas type production
functions. The law governing labour supply is

$$L_t = L_0(1 + \nu)^t,$$

for positive values of ν and L_0, where ν is the rate of growth of the population
and L_0 is the starting population. It is obvious that the form of the labour
supply curve is of the same type as in the case of no growth, but for the upper
asymptote, which increases as time passes, the asymptotes being measured by
the values taken by L_t.

10.2 No R&D Activity

10.2.1 First COD-Simulation

The data for the first COD simulation are the same as in the second COD
simulation in Chapter 7:

$$\theta = 2, \quad \alpha = 0.2, \quad \beta = 0.5, \quad \delta = 0.2, \quad K_0 = 250, \quad w_0 = 5,$$

to which values we add new ones for a steady increasing population, i.e.:

$$P_0 = 100, \quad \nu = 0.005.$$

The rate of population growth, ν, chosen to take the value 0.5%, is in some
sense half way between the annual rate of population increase in many rich
countries, which takes values near zero, and the rate in very poor countries,

which is frequently greater than 1%. To give an idea of total population growth at the end of the chosen time horizon, i.e. $n = 120$ periods, we have $P_{120} = 100(1 + 0.005)^{120} = 182$. Of course, the order of magnitude of this result depends on the length of the time period; if, as we have tacitly assumed, each period lasts one month, then the time horizon embraces ten years and the chosen rate of population growth must be considered extremely high. If each period lasts one year, then the time horizon becomes 120 years and the growth rate is not very high.

We report here only Figures COD1.1–5 generated by the program, because there are no marked differences between them and the figures generated for the corresponding case of zero population growth. In particular, Figure COD1.4 shows that labour supply is upper limited by a value that is less than 30, so that the fact that, starting from $P_0 = 100$, population increases steadily has no impact on the economy, which behaves the same as in the case of a stationary population. This is due to the wage rate, which is so low as to severely limit labour supply. Thus, labour demand takes the same values as in the stationary population case.

Total consumption takes the value $CT_{120} = 6965$. Of course, comparing this value to that generated in the analogous simulation under stationary population, we again observe the value $CT_{120} = 6965$, which now must be shared among a greater number of individuals. Thus, merely increasing population, and correspondingly the labour force, does not necessarily increase total consumption, and reduces per capita consumption. In strict economic

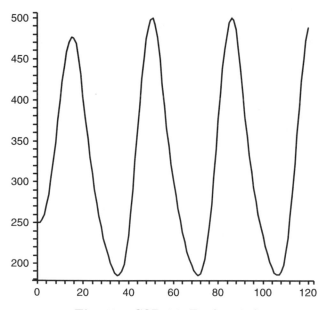

Fig. 10.1 COD 1.1: Total capital

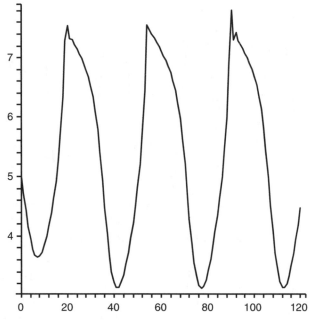

Fig. 10.2 COD 1.2: Wage rate

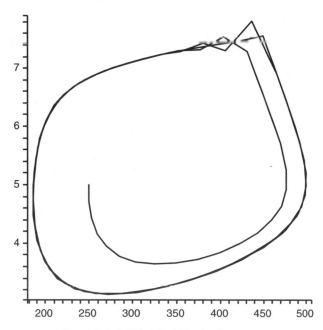

Fig. 10.3 COD 1.3: (K, w)-phase space

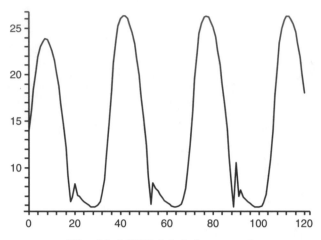

Fig. 10.4 COD 1.4: Labour supply

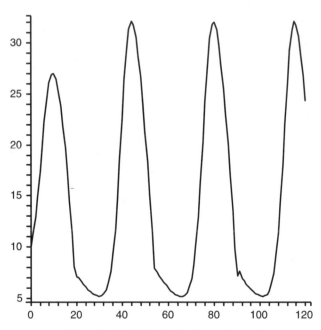

Fig. 10.5 COD 1.5: Labour demand

terms, this means that, on average, the population enjoys less material welfare. Of course, in the poor countries of the third world the burden of population very often severely limits the possibilities for economic growth, at least with the current organization of the poorest economies.

A similar result is obtained if we implement a simulation in which the only modified value is $\nu = 0.01$, double the previous value. Again, total consumption takes the same value, and population is even more materially impoverished than in the preceding case.

10.3 Positive R&D Expenditure

10.3.1 Second COD-Simulation

Assume that, all else remaining the same, in every period a small fraction of profits is devoted to R&D, with the aim of increasing, period by period, the total productivity parameter, θ. The second COD simulation is implemented by means of the first COD simulation values, except for the coefficient applied to the profit needed to generate R&D expenditure, chosen as $\epsilon = 0.01$. The coefficients of the productivity function are, as in previous chapters, $c = 0.1$ and $d = 0.5$.

Total consumption, from Figure COD2.14, is $CT_{120} \approx 1.06 \times 10^6$, a value many times higher than under no R&D activity: even investing a small fraction of profits to improve existing technologies, provides major benefits.

From Figure COD2.1 it can be seen that, after 30 periods, when capital increases very slowly, this state variable starts growing at an accelerating rate, up to the end of the horizon. The wage rate time path, as depicted in Figure COD2.2, steadily increases only from period 40. The phase diagram confirms that the state variables increase regularly after a short starting time interval:

Figure COD2.4 shows a qualitatively different labour supply evolution over time: it is subject to a sequence of mild and trend increasing oscillations between periods 1 and 20, after which it increases steadily. Labour demand, as depicted in Figure COD2.5, experiences two wide oscillations, whose mean values are strongly increasing.

Looking at the time behaviour of GDP, represented in Figure COD2.6, it has the same growth dynamics as capital: it starts increasing at an increasing rate from period 35. The same type of evolution is experienced by total profits, as can be seen from Figure COD2.7. Per capita production and production per worker evolve in similar ways (see Figures COD2.8–9): after slight initial oscillations, from period 45 they increase steadily. Their similarity is explained by the employment ratio, after period 16, being permanently equal to 1.

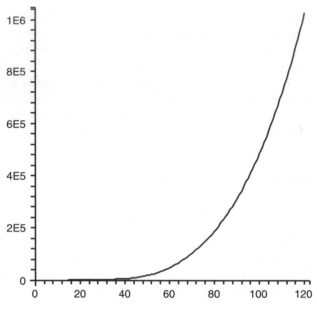

Fig. 10.6 COD 2.14: Total consumption

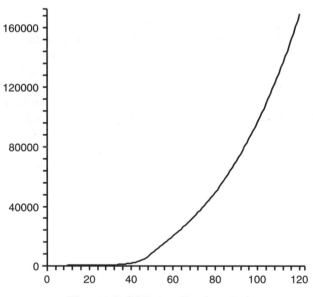

Fig. 10.7 COD 2.1: Total capital

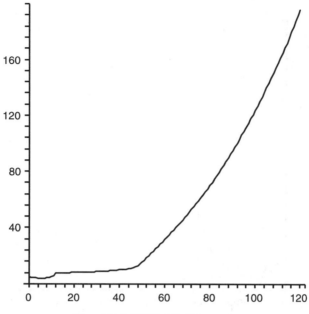

Fig. 10.8 COD 2.2: Wage rate

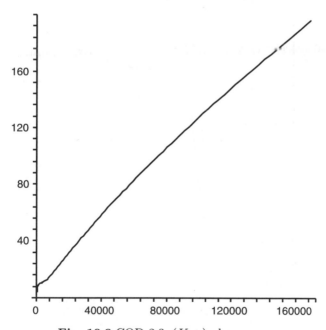

Fig. 10.9 COD 2.3: (K, w)-phase space

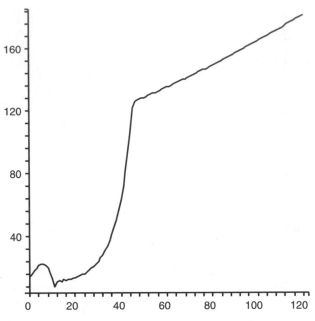

Fig. 10.10 COD 2.4: Labour supply

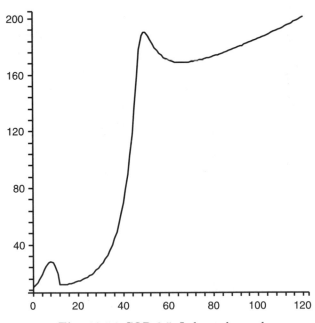

Fig. 10.11 COD 2.5: Labour demand

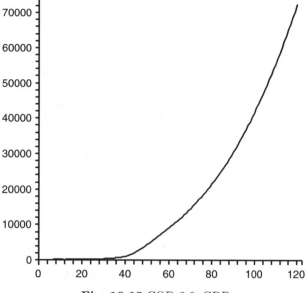

Fig. 10.12 COD 2.6: GDP

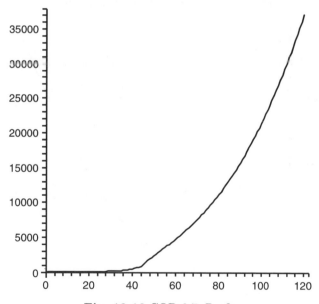

Fig. 10.13 COD 2.7: Profits

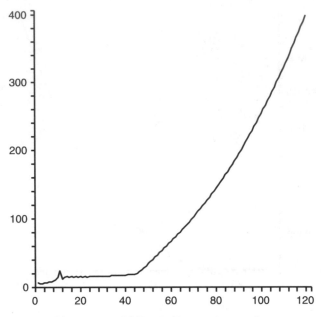

Fig. 10.14 COD 2.8: Pro capite product

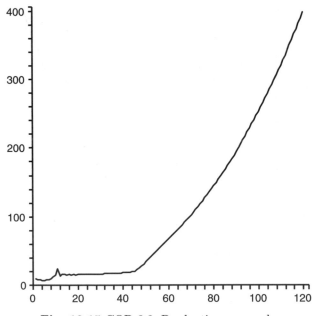

Fig. 10.15 COD 2.9: Production per worker

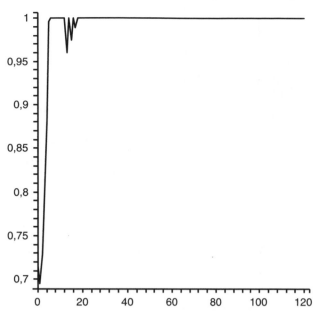

Fig. 10.16 COD 2.10: Employment ratio

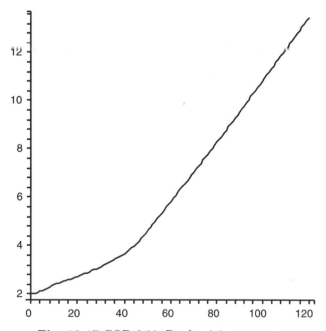

Fig. 10.17 COD 2.11: Productivity parameter

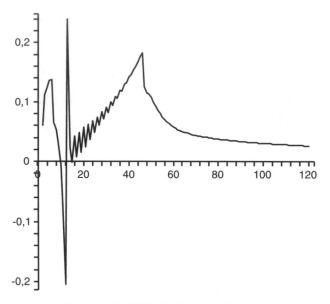

Fig. 10.18 COD 2.12: Rate of growth

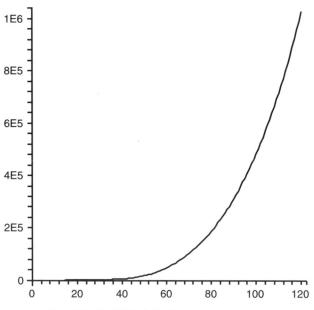

Fig. 10.19 COD 2.14: Total consumption

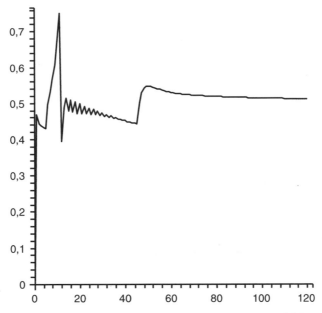

Fig. 10.20 COD 2.15: Percentage of profits in GDP

The employment ratio shows different and interesting behaviour over time, as depicted in Figure COD2.10; it oscillates from period 10 to 16, with in creasing bottom values, while the top value is 1 from period 16 on, manifesting permanent full employment. The productivity parameter, Figure COD2.11, increases at an increasing rate, from its starting value of 2 to a final value greater than 13.

In terms of rate of growth of the economy, Figure COD2.12 shows that its time path is quite irregular: it shows a very pronounced oscillation in the first 15 periods, followed by frequent and increasing oscillations up to period 47, after which it decreases steadily to the end of the selected horizon.

Finally, rate of growth and percentage of profits in GDP show qualitatively similar time paths (Figures COD2.12, 2.15).

10.3.2 Third COD-Simulation

The third and last simulation in this series modifies the value of the adjustment velocity of the wage rate. Now the choice is $\alpha = 0.4$, everything else remaining the same as in the second COD simulation. As expected, based on the simulations reported in the previous chapters, oscillations are more numerous and severe than in the second simulation. More specifically, for wage rate very mild cycles occur between periods 10 and 70, shown in Figure COD3.2, while, from period 50 on, capital increases steadily and at an increasing rate (Figure COD3.1). Of course, the phase space in the next figure, after a start-

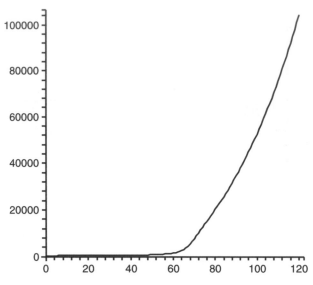

Fig. 10.21 COD 3.1: Total capital

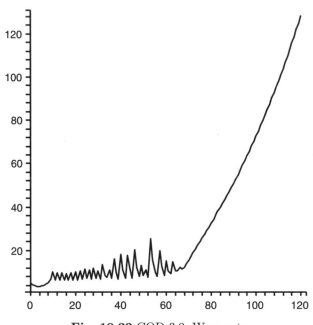

Fig. 10.22 COD 3.2: Wage rate

ing time interval of turbulence, shows steady growth for both capital and wage rate.

In Figure COD3.4, periods 8 to 68 show labour supply is subject to very irregular cycles, whose top values have a tendency to increase over time. From period 68 on, the increase becomes regular up to the end of the time horizon. Labour demand also oscillates irregularly up to period 68 (see Figure COD3.5), after which time it shows regular behaviour. With respect to the other variables, it should be noted, as depicted in Figures COD3.8–9, that per capita production and production per worker show similar paths, which oscillate somewhat irregularly between periods 10 and 66, and then increase steadily.

Figure COD3.10 clearly depicts an employment ratio that, for the same time interval (periods 10 to 68) oscillates very irregularly between 8% and full employment; of course, the amplitudes of these oscillations are completely unrealistic in terms of a real economy.

Also the rate of growth, depicted in Figure COD3.12, oscillates very dramatically up to period 68, before slightly decreasing to a value of about 4% per period.[1]

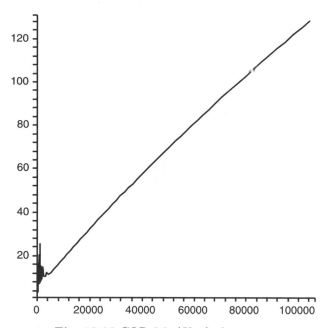

Fig. 10.23 COD 3.3: (K, w)-phase space

---

[1] If every period lasts one year then this value is very reasonable, and in line with the data collected for many real economies; but if every period lasts only one month a 4% value is beyond the possibilities of any real world economy.

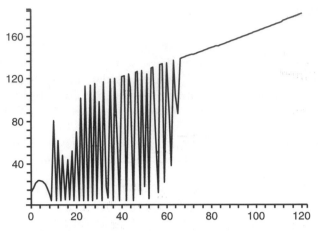

Fig. 10.24 COD 3.4: Labour supply

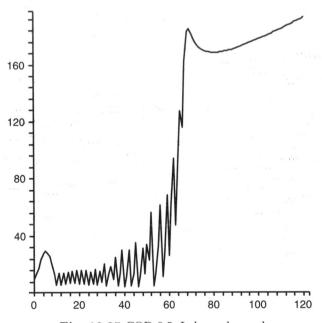

Fig. 10.25 COD 3.5: Labour demand

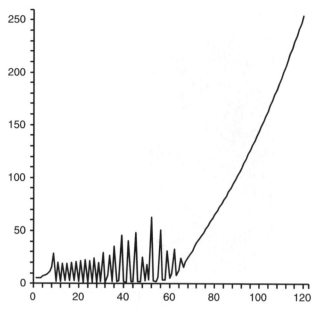

Fig. 10.26 COD 3.8: Pro capite product

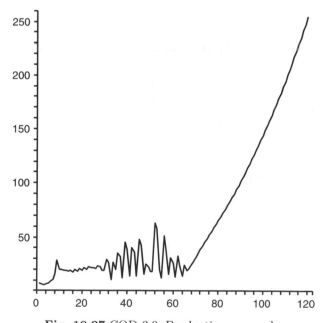

Fig. 10.27 COD 3.9: Production per worker

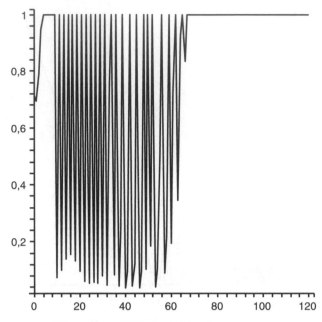

Fig. 10.28 COD 3.10: Employment ratio

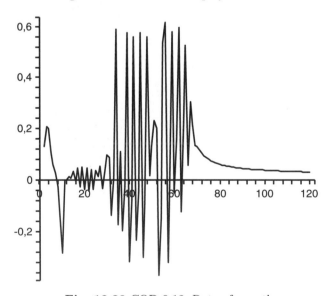

Fig. 10.29 COD 3.12: Rate of growth

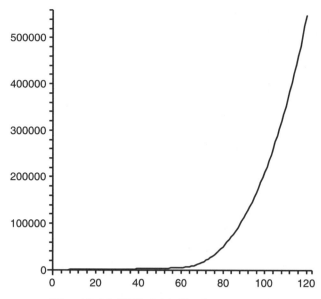

Fig. 10.30 COD 3.14: Total consumption

To conclude, Figure COD3.14 shows that total consumption starts increasing very rapidly from period 60 on, and reaches $CT_{120} \approx 540000$ at the end of the time horizon. This value is about half that obtained in the second COD simulation; once more, increasing the velocity of adjustment of the wage rate and subjecting the economy to many short cycles, has a very negative effect on material welfare.

11

Logistic Growing Population

11.1 Preliminary

As before, simulations are implemented for Cobb–Douglas production functions. Before presenting the results of the simulations implemented for the logistic growing population case, let us consider two quite different time evolutions of the logistic law, obtained by specific parameter values selected for equation (1.4) presented in Chapter 2.

In the first the evolution is obtained by choosing the following parameter values: $\zeta = 2.5$ and $\xi = 0.0125$. Thus, the logistic equation reads

$$P_{t+1} = 2.5P_t - 0.0125P_t^2. \tag{1.1}$$

If we take $P_0 = 100$, and consider a time span of 120 periods then the previous equation generates the following time path: It is clear that, after some rapidly fading oscillations, P_t takes a stationary value of $P^* = 120$, and all P_t values belong to the compact interval $[0, 125]$.

In the second illustration, we consider the following values: $\zeta = 4, \xi = 0.008$ with the same starting population, $P_0 = 100$. The new time path of P_t is depicted in the next figure:[1]

It is quite evident that in this case population oscillates almost randomly between a value that is extremely small, approximately 0.0105, and the value 500. Of course, no human population has ever experienced similar wild oscillations. Thus, the preceding parameter values appear completely unrealistic, when applied to human population growth. The simulations in this chapter are implemented by taking the parameter values corresponding to the first of the previous two examples, i.e. to equation (1.1) above.

---

[1] As noted in Chapter 2, the time behaviour for P_t is the same for a much longer time horizon, indeed for any time horizon.

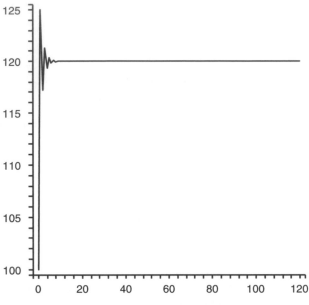

Fig. 11.1. Logistic population 1

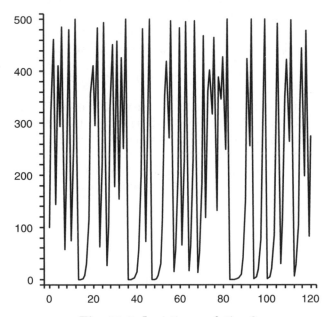

Fig. 11.2. Logistic population 2

11.2 No R&D Activity

11.2.1 First COD-Simulation

We choose the same values as in the first simulation in Chapter 7, but for $\alpha = 0.2$ and for the equation governing population growth, which now follows law (1.1). As reported in Section 1, this equation generates values P_t belonging to the compact interval $[0, 125]$, rapidly converging to the stationary value $P^* = 120$. Thus, any P_0 in this interval is an allowable starting value, and this is particularly true for the chosen value $P_0 = 100$.

The simulation shows that the state variables undergo circa three and a half cycles, which of course have no trend, as pictured in Figures CODL1.1–2:

This trend-stationarity can be seen in Figure CODL1.3, which depicts the phase space: While the state variables cycle follows a fairly even pattern, other variables oscillate more irregularly. For example, Figure CODL1.4 shows that within every cycle for labour supply, there are small time intervals in which changes are somewhat irregular. This is true also for per capita production, plotted in Figure CODL1.8, and production per worker, depicted in Figure CODL1.9. The employment ratio is also subject to irregular changes (Figure CODL1.10), and full employment is achieved for about one third of the time horizon.

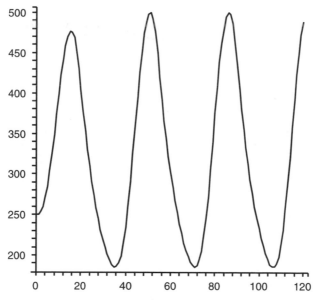

Fig. 11.3 CODL 1.1: Total capital

The most irregularly cycles in the time series are for growth rate, plotted in Figure CODL1.12. Its values are within a very wide range from approximately

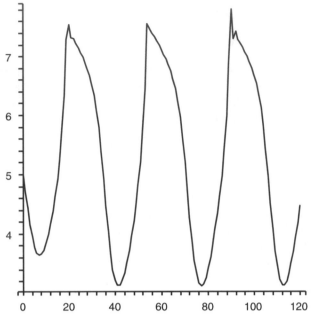

Fig. 11.4 CODL 1.2: Wage rate

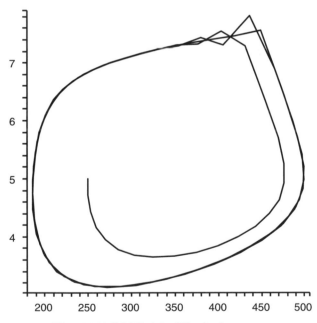

Fig. 11.5 CODL 1.3: (K, w)-phase space

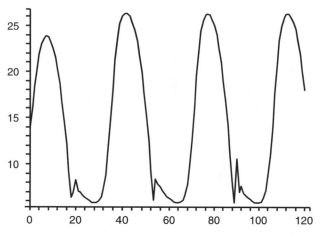

Fig. 11.6 CODL 1.4: Labour supply

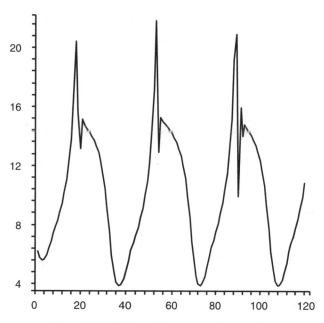

Fig. 11.7 CODL 1.8: Pro capite product

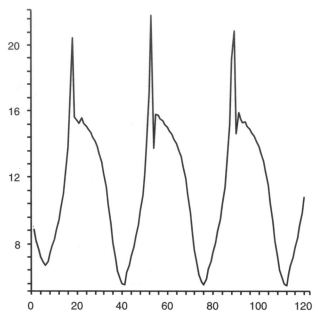

Fig. 11.8 CODL 1.9: Production per worker

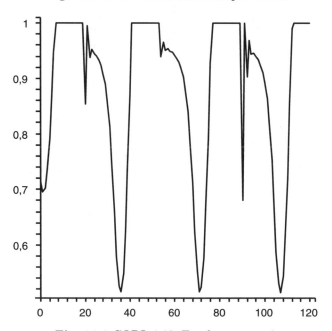

Fig. 11.9 CODL 1.10: Employment ratio

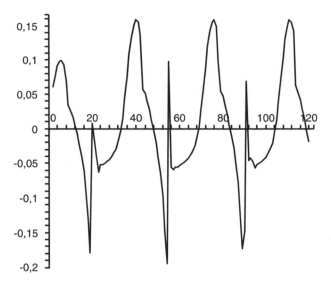

Fig. 11.10 CODL 1.12: Rate of growth

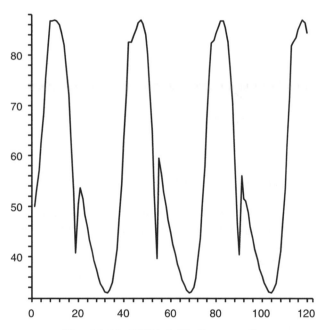

Fig. 11.11 CODL 1.13: Consumption

−0.19 to +0.16; negative values and positive values obtain for about the same number of periods. Of course, the average rate of growth is zero.

Consumption too, presented in Figure CODL1.13, experiences irregular cycles, while total consumption, plotted in Figure CODL1.14, grows fairly steadily and at the end of the horizon takes the value $CT_{120} \approx 6960$.

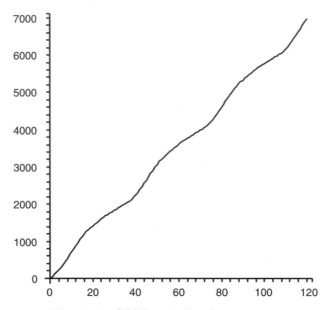

Fig. 11.12 CODL 1.14: Total consumption

11.2.2 Second COD-Simulation

Despite the fact that we are working in discrete time, we now implement some simulations in which population, and hence labour supply, while growing in discrete time, follow the same logistic law as when time is considered as a continuous variable. This choice allows us to compare directly the results of the following simulations with those implemented in Chapter 10 when population[2] grows at a steady state. Thus, the law governing the time evolution of labour supply is similar to that presented in Section 1.1 of Chapter 2. Specifically, let us consider the law expressed by the function

$$P_t = \frac{600}{5 + 0.95^t} \qquad (t = 0, 1, 2, \ldots). \tag{2.1}$$

---

[2] Of course, the assumption here is that the labour supply ceiling is subject to the same time evolution.

Function (2.1) verifies $P_0 = 100$ and $P^* = 120$. In particular, we have $P_{120} = 119.949$, which is practically the same final end value, 120, taken by labour supply in the simulations in Chapter 10.

We implement this simulation applying mostly the same values as in the first simulation in this chapter, with the exception of labour force, which increases in time according to function (2.1). The results are summarized in Figures CODL2.1–15. In particular, Figures CODL2.1–3 show that the state variables have the same qualitative trajectories, which are rapidly increasing towards their asymptotes:

The other main variables are summarized in Figures CODL2.4–9.

Apart from labour demand (Figure CODL2.5), and with the exception of a short starting transitory phase, all the time paths show increasing trends to their respective stationary values.

This is true for the employment ratio also (Figure CODL2.10), showing that the ceiling value is quickly achieved and thereafter is maintained.

The rate of growth, depicted in Figure CODL2.12, after some very wide oscillations, very quickly reaches its stationary value, which is equal to zero. Figure 2.14 shows that total consumption at the end of the horizon takes the value $CT_{120} \approx 576000$, which is more than eight times the value in the previous simulation. Again, the explanation is that in this simulation the stationary values are reached gradually, while in the preceding one cycles occur continuously.

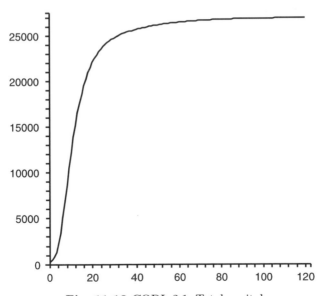

Fig. 11.13 CODL 2.1: Total capital

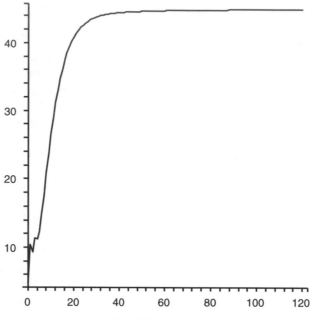

Fig. 11.14 CODL 2.2: Wage rate

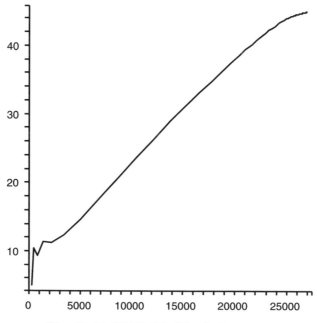

Fig. 11.15 CODL 2.3: (K, w)-phase space

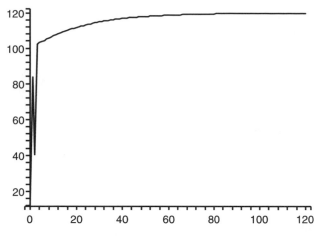

Fig. 11.16 CODL 2.4: Labour supply

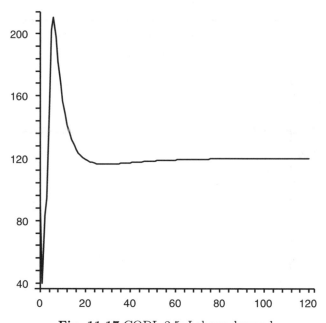

Fig. 11.17 CODL 2.5: Labour demand

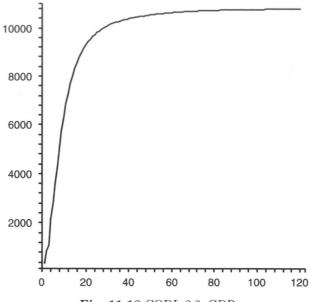

Fig. 11.18 CODL 2.6: GDP

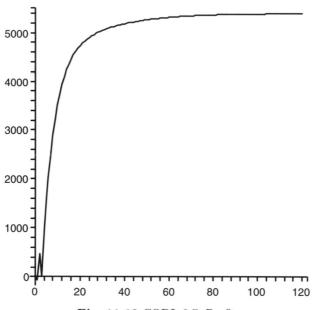

Fig. 11.19 CODL 2.7: Profits

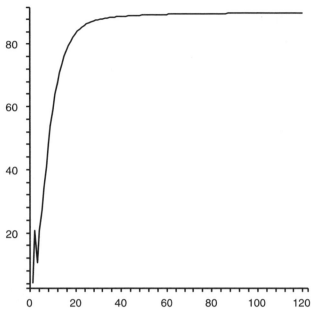

Fig. 11.20 CODL 2.8: Pro capite product

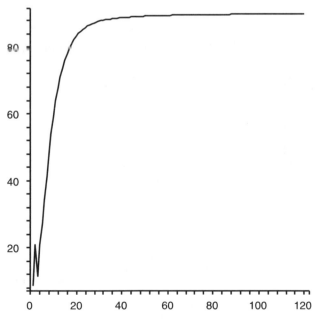

Fig. 11.21 CODL 2.9: Production per worker

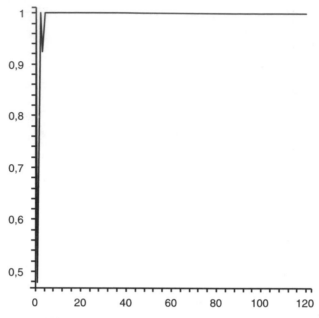

Fig. 11.22 CODL 2.10: Employment ratio

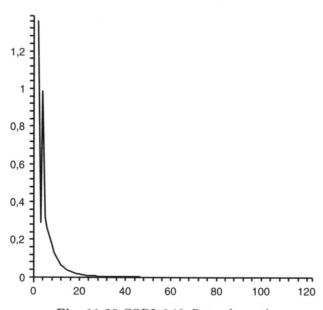

Fig. 11.23 CODL 2.12: Rate of growth

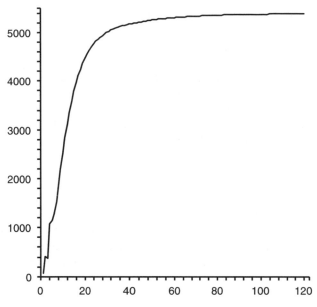

Fig. 11.24 CODL 2.13: Consumption

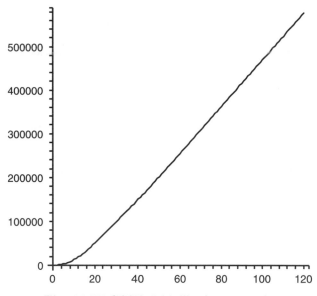

Fig. 11.25 CODL 2.14: Total consumption

11.3 Positive R&D Expenditure

11.3.1 Third COD-Simulation

The next simulation, CODL3, includes R&D activity alongside the same parameters and functions as in the first CODL-simulation.

Fraction $\epsilon = 0.01$ of every period profit is devoted to R&D, while the total productivity production function is still expressed by $f(X^r) = c(X^r)^d$, where X^r denotes labour input in R&D activity, with values of $c = 0.1$ and $d = 0.5$, namely:

$$f(X^r) = 0.1(X^r)^{0.5}.$$

The effect of R&D activity on the material welfare can be quickly assessed; total consumption takes the value $CT_{120} \approx 2.5 \times 10^6$, as depicted in Figure CODL3.14. Of course, this result appears impressive when compared to the value obtained in the simulation CODL1. Again it shows that it is very rewarding to devote a small quota of profits to investment in R&D activity, when the time horizon is sufficiently extended. This result is well demonstrated if we consider the productivity parameter, depicted in Figure CODL3.11, whose value equals $\theta_{120} = 18$, or three times its starting value of $\theta_0 = 6$, at the end of the time horizon.

Figures CODL3.1–3 present the state variables, which are self explanatory. They manifest steady growth, as does the economic quantity shown in Figure CODL3.4, except for a short transitory phase at the start, while labour

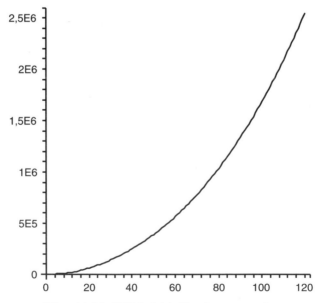

Fig. 11.26 CODL 3.14: Total consumption

demand, depicted in Figure CODL3.5, after a huge oscillation becomes almost stationary, gradually decreasing to the maximum labour supply value.

The next two Figures CODL3.6–7, again show a marked tendency to steady growth, with a very short transitory phase:

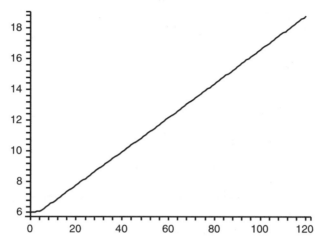

Fig. 11.27 CODL 3.11: Productivity parameter

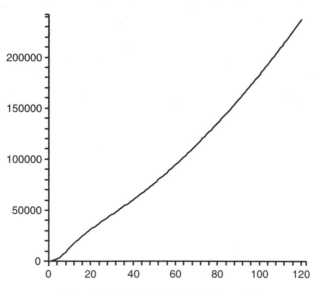

Fig. 11.28 CODL 3.1: Total capital

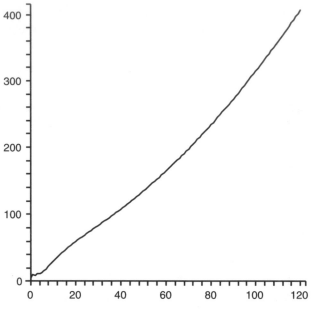

Fig. 11.29 CODL 3.2: Wage rate

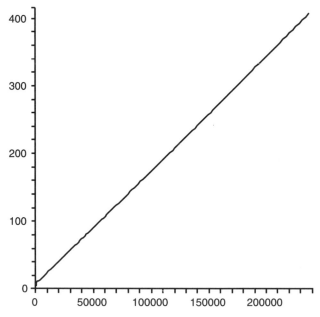

Fig. 11.30 CODL 3.3: (K, w)-phase space

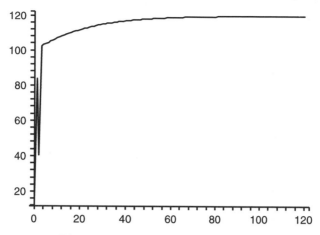

Fig. 11.31 CODL 3.4: Labour supply

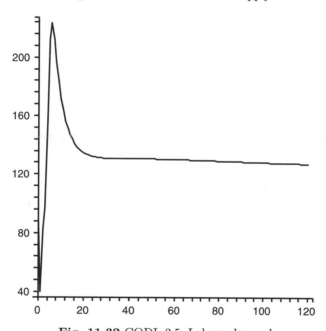

Fig. 11.32 CODL 3.5: Labour demand

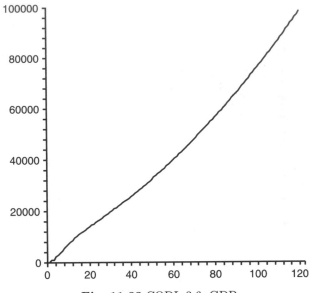

Fig. 11.33 CODL 3.6: GDP

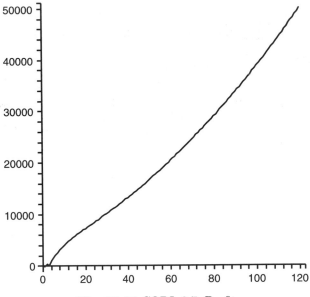

Fig. 11.34 CODL 3.7: Profits

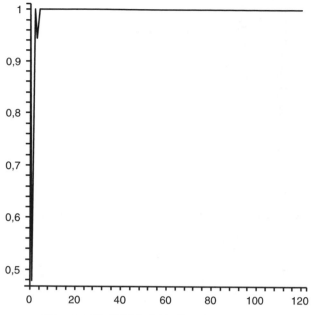

Fig. 11.35 CODL 3.10: Employment ratio

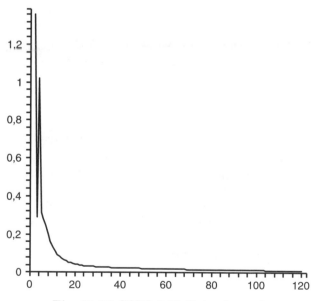

Fig. 11.36 CODL 3.12: Rate of growth

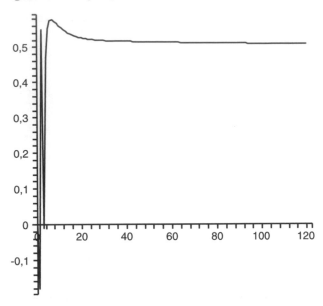

Fig. 11.37 CODL 3.15: Percentage of profits in GDP

The scenario is a bit different for the variables for employment ratio, depicted in Figure CODL3.10, rate of growth, plotted in Figure CODL3.12, and percentage of profits on GDP, depicted in Figure CODL3.15. All these quantities are subject to irregular changes in the initial periods, but then move steadily.

11.3.2 Fourth COD-Simulation

The only difference with respect to Simulation CODL3, is in relation to the R&D expenditure parameter whose value increases to $\epsilon = 0.02$, i.e. 2% of the profit in every period is devoted to R&D activity. Qualitatively, these results, whose presentation is limited to the state variables depicted in Figures CODL4.1–3, look the same as in the preceding simulation. Of course, total consumption, shown in Figure CODL4.14, now has the value $CT_{120} \approx 3.8 \times 10^6$, which, when compared to the number obtained in the third simulation, again demonstrates the importance, at least in the long run, of a proportionate percentage increase in R&D expenditure.

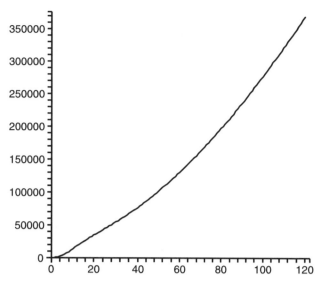

Fig. 11.38 CODL 4.1: Total capital

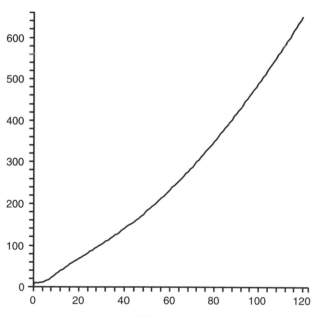

Fig. 11.39 CODL 4.2: Wage rate

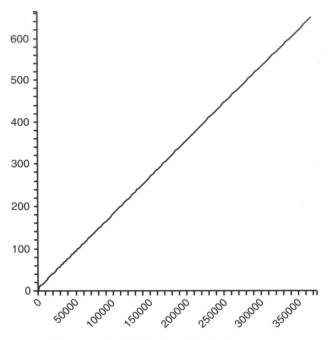

Fig. 11.40 CODL 4.3: (K, w)-phase space

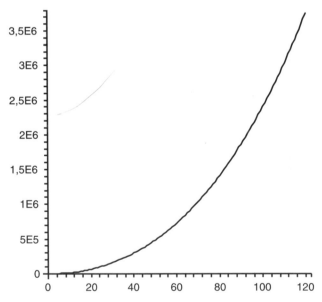

Fig. 11.41 CODL 4.14: Total consumption

11.4 Logistic Population Growth: A Caveat

In discrete time, and according to the values given to the parameters, application of the logistic law can produce very different types of results, as we showed in Chapter 2, from steady growth to chaotic behaviour. Applied to the case of human population dynamics, where in real world situations[3] populations change only very slightly from year to year, the logistic law can provide a satisfactory approximation of a real world situation only when parameters are chosen that render yearly rates of change very low, as in the third and fourth simulations in this chapter. But in this case, if the time horizon is not extended to thousands of periods, logistic law behaves more or less like steady growth law, employed in the experiments in Chapter 10, because the absence of an upper asymptote in the steady growth law has a strong influence on the economy only in the very long run. It is only when secular time horizons are considered that logistic law behaves very differently from steady state growth law.

---

[3] Only in very exceptional situations, e.g., during the type of countrywide plagues as occurred during the Middle Ages, which resulted in short time intervals when populations were severely reduced.

Effects of Public Expenditure

12.1 Preliminary

The last set of simulations presented in the following pages, takes account of the impact of public expenditure, whose aim, as stated in Chapter 6, is the production of infrastructure,[1] on the performance of the economy, and especially on its growth. The model to be implemented was presented in Chapter 6, and we consider simulations for the case of a stationary population, and thus a stationary labour supply, whose value is $P = L = 100$, and for a Cobb–Douglas production function.

Because the amount of infrastructure, Z, acts on the production of GDP like a productivity parameter, θ, there is likely no possible stationary state for the economy since, in every period, there is an increase in infrastructure input, which means an increase in the productivity of both labour and capital.[2]

12.2 Zero R&D Activity

Let us start by considering an economy where there is no R&D activity, in order to isolate the impact of public expenditure alone on the considered model economy.

---

[1] It should be remembered that here infrastructure includes everything financed by public expenditure that has a positive impact on the economy.

[2] However, building infrastructure can produce a conflict with private investment, and therefore with the growth of capital. This means that some simulations present a time path with growth rate values that approach zero towards the end of the chosen horizon.

12.2.1 First CODPE-Simulation

The parameter values chosen are the same as in the first COD simulation proposed in Chapter 7, i.e.

$$\alpha = 0.1, \quad \theta = 6, \quad \beta = 0.5, \quad \delta = 0.2,$$

while the starting values assigned to the state variables are

$$K_0 = 250, \quad w_0 = 5.$$

The new parameters relating to taxation, public expenditure, and infrastructure, are:

$$\tau = 0.3, \quad \kappa = 0.00001, \quad \eta = 0.1.$$

Let us also assume $Z_0 = 1.$[3] The low values given to η and κ are justified by the fact that it was assumed that one unit of public expenditure generates κ units of infrastructure. Since the infrastructure function is $Z_t^{0.1}$, with marginal productivity $0.1 Z_t^{-0.9}$, this means that in a sense "too much" infrastructure is unproductive,[4] so that this type of Keynesian policy, i.e. to build infrastructures, i.e. public works, is only partially effective in terms of economic growth.

The set of figures produced by the simulation in question are reported in the pages that follow, and the corresponding time series are compared to the analogous time series produced by means of the first COD simulation presented in Chapter 7.

Figures CODPE 1.1–3, which are compared to the corresponding three figures in the first simulation in Chapter 7, show that both capital endowment and wage rate, after two starting phases when there are some slight oscillations, increase in value steadily up to the end of the time horizon.

As the next two figures show, labour supply quickly reaches its peak value of 100, while labour demand initially decreases and then rapidly increases to reach a value that is more than twice the maximum possible value, i.e. 100, then decreases steadily to the maximum possible value. At the end of the horizon, GDP is $Y_{120} \approx 8000$, which is a bit less than the corresponding value shown in Figure COD 1.6 in Chapter 7; of course, as already mentioned, depending on the specific values given to the parameters of the infrastructure function, this result seems to imply some limitation on the impact of building infrastructures on the growth of the economy.

Per capita production and production per worker, in Figures CODPE 1.8–9, take the same values along the chosen horizon, since full employment

---

[3] This value is chosen to allow comparison of the results of the simulations in this chapter with the ones when no infrastructure is considered, or, better, when the infrastructure value is always $Z_t = 1$.

[4] In real economies infrastructures are normally deficient; thus, this situation is unlikely to occur.

of labour, as previously stated, is quickly obtained. Moreover, after a short transitory phase, the employment ratio is permanently equal to 100%, as shown in Figure CODPE 1.10, with the exception of a slight contraction between periods 35 and 40. The rate of growth of the economy, shown in Figure CODPE 1.12, in the first two periods takes an impossible peak value, and then, from period 3 onward, rapidly decreases to a value that is approximately equal to 0.002.[5] From Figure CODPE 1.14 we see that total consumption at the end of the chosen time horizon is $CT_{120} \approx 380000$, a value significantly less than the corresponding value reported by the first simulation in Chapter 7. Figure CODPE 1.15 shows that the post tax profit rate is oscillating, and after 30 periods is less than 40%. To conclude this simulation, Figure CODPE 1.16 presents the time path for infrastructure, showing that at the end of the time horizon the quantity of infrastructure has more than doubled its starting value; but its impact on the growth of the economy is negligible.

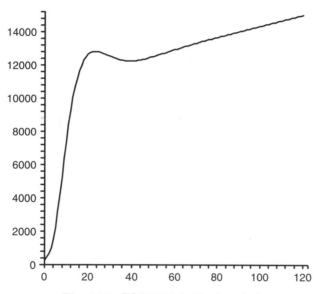

Fig. 12.1 CODPE 1.1: Total capital

---

[5] If we consider a longer time horizon, e.g. $n = 200$, we can confirm that the rate of growth continues to decrease, but does not reach zero.

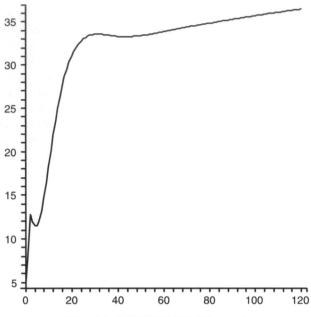

Fig. 12.2 CODPE 1.2: Wage rate

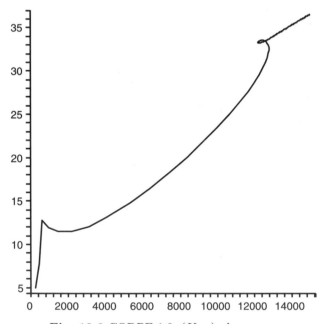

Fig. 12.3 CODPE 1.3: (K, w)-phase space

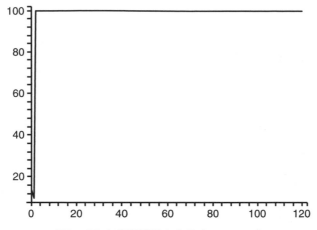

Fig. 12.4 CODPE 1.4: Labour supply

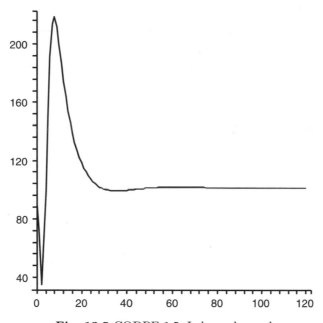

Fig. 12.5 CODPE 1.5: Labour demand

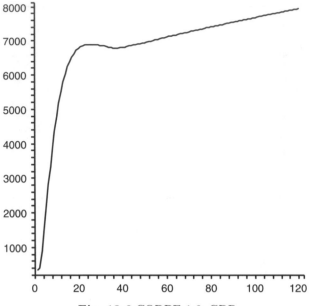

Fig. 12.6 CODPE 1.6: GDP

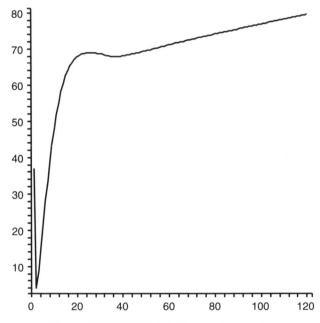

Fig. 12.7 CODPE 1.8: Pro capite product

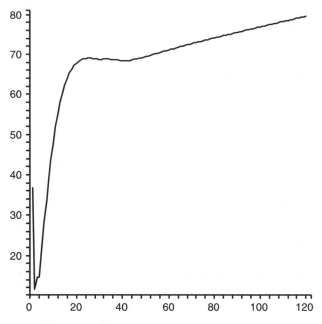

Fig. 12.8 CODPE 1.9: Production per worker

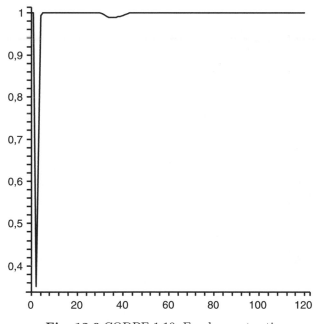

Fig. 12.9 CODPE 1.10: Employment ratio

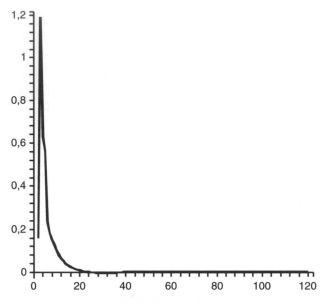

Fig. 12.10 CODPE 1.12: Rate of growth

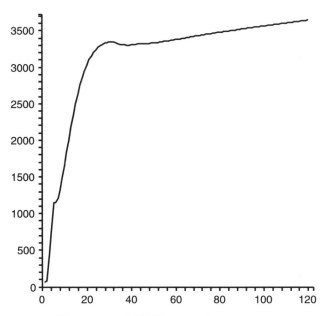

Fig. 12.11 CODPE 1.13: Consumption

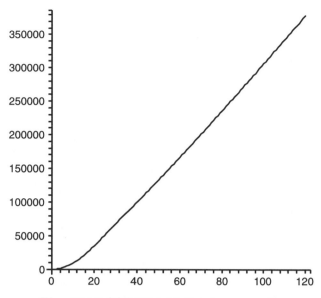

Fig. 12.12 CODPE 1.14: Total consumption

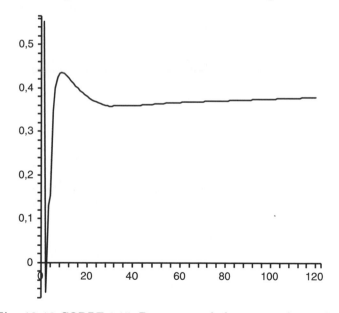

Fig. 12.13 CODPE 1.15: Percentage of after tax profits on GDP

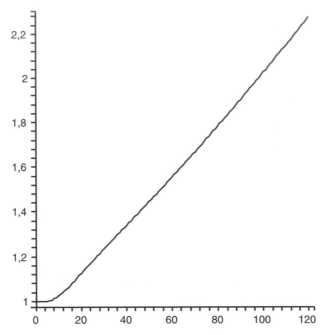

Fig. 12.14 CODPE 1.16: Infrastructure

12.2.2 Second CODPE-Simulation

To verify the impact of public expenditure, the productivity parameter, κ, of public expenditure is doubled, and thus takes the value $\kappa = 0.00002$. The results of this simulation are qualitatively very similar to those produced by the first simulation. But Figures 2.14 and 2.16 show that the economy performs more efficiently in terms of total consumption, due to the increased productivity of public expenditure. Total consumption is $CT_{120} = 400000$, or 15% greater than the same value in the preceding simulation, while the amount of infrastructure at the end of the horizon is, $Z_{120} \approx 3.9$, significantly greater than the quantity obtained in the preceding simulation.

As a variant, we can assume that instead of changing the parameter κ, we double η; thus, $\kappa = 0.00001$, $\eta = 0.2$. This variant of the preceding simulation shows that the time behaviour of the main variables does not change with respect to the previous two simulations; so we need only present the figures corresponding to the two previous ones: The figure for total consumption shows that its end value is comparable to that obtained in the preceding simulation, while the figure on infrastructure shows that its final amount is comparable to that obtained in the first simulation, meaning that now this input is more productive in terms of the material welfare index, CT_{120}, than the infrastructure in the preceding simulation.

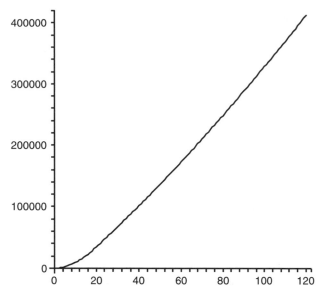

Fig. 12.15 CODPE 2.14: Total consumption

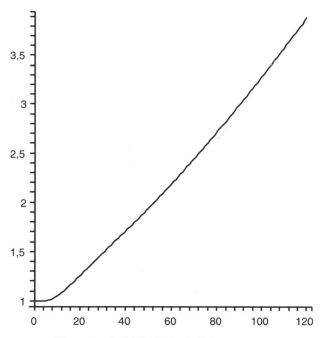

Fig. 12.16 CODPE 2.16: Infrastructure

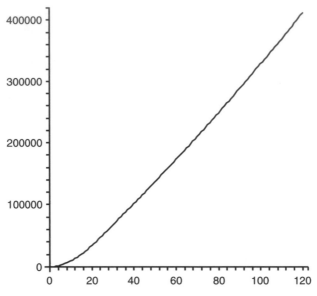

Fig. 12.17 CODPE 2a.14: Total consumption

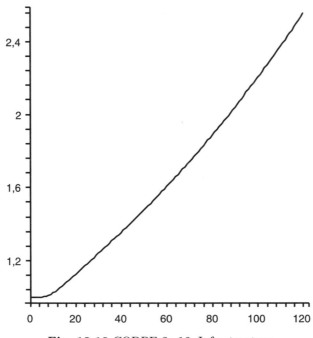

Fig. 12.18 CODPE 2a.16: Infrastructure

12.3 Positive R&D Expenditure

Let us now implement two simulations with positive expenditure on R&D. With the objective of assessing the potential of public expenditure with respect to R&D expenditure, let us consider a total expenditure, including R&D and infrastructure, that is equal to the public expenditure, G, considered in the first simulation in this chapter. In essence, this amounts to assuming that the government gives back to firms a fraction of the taxes it levies, with the proviso that the corresponding sum is spent completely on R&D, in order to increase the productivity of both labour and capital, as measured by the parameter θ. Thus, remembering relations (2.3) and (2.4) in Chapter 6, in every period let us consider, for $t = 1, 2, \ldots, 120$,

$$G_t = \tau \pi_{t-1} = Z_t/\kappa + R_t = Z_t/\kappa + \epsilon \max\{0, \pi_{t-1}\}.$$

That is, we assume gross profits to be positive, from the previous relation we have

$$Z_t = \kappa(\tau - \epsilon)\pi_{t-1},$$

which value is surely positive, since the time constant rate of taxation, $\tau = 0.3$, is much greater than the value assigned to ϵ in the third and fourth simulations below.

12.3.1 Third CODPE-Simulation

The data chosen to implement this simulation, assuming positive R&D and public expenditure, are the same as in the first simulation in this chapter, but instead of $\epsilon = 0$, we choose $\epsilon = 0.01$, and assume $c = 0.1$, $d = 0.5$ in the production function of θ, as in the fourth simulation in Chapter 7. The parameter values thus become

$$\alpha = 0.1, \quad \beta = 0.5, \quad \delta = 0.2, \quad \epsilon = 0.01, \quad c = 0.1, \quad d = 0.5,$$

$$\tau = 0.3, \quad \kappa = 0.00001, \quad \eta = 0.1,$$

and the starting values are

$$K_0 = 250, \quad w_0 = 5, \quad \theta_0 = 6, \quad Z_0 = 1.$$

The following figures summarize the results of the simulation. In general, it can be seen that both the final amount of capital, $K_{120} \approx 240000$, and the last period wage rate, $w_{120} \approx 440$, seem to take unusually high values, shown in Figures CODPE 3.1-2, when compared to their starting values.[6] With respect to wage rate, this seemingly anomalous result can be imputed to the permanent high demand for labour with respect to its limited supply, equal to 100 units, as depicted in Figures 3.4–5.

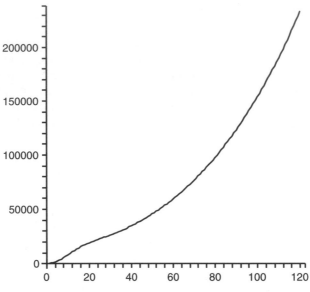

Fig. 12.19 CODPE 3.1: Total capital

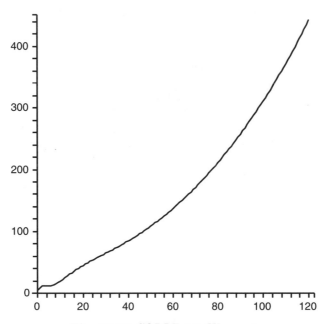

Fig. 12.20 CODPE 3.2: Wage rate

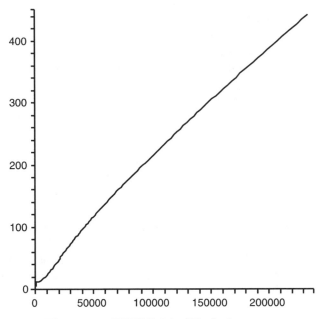

Fig. 12.21 CODPE 3.3: (K, w)-phase space

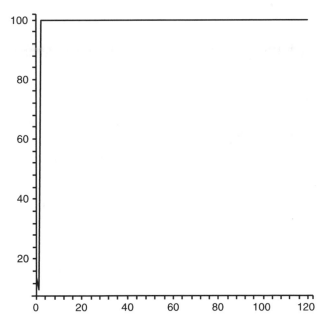

Fig. 12.22 CODPE 3.4: Labour supply

From Figures CODPE 3.6–16 it can be seen that, apart from the first five periods for some time series, all these graphs are smooth; it is also interesting that the rate of growth, shown in Figure CODPE3.12, decreases steadily towards very low values, while remaining positive. One possible explanation is that the wage rate is so high that consumption absorbs a consistent fraction of GDP, thus compressing the quota of GDP devoted to R&D and public expenditure. But Figures CODPE3.6 and 3.7 show that before tax profits are a consistent fraction, about 60%, of GDP.

We next look at total consumption at the end of the horizon. Figure CODPE 3.14 shows that this value amounts to $CT_{120} \approx 2 \times 10^6$, a value many times greater than the corresponding values in the other simulations in this chapter. Comparing this value to the corresponding, $CT_{120} \approx 380000$, obtained by implementing the first simulation in this chapter, the effectiveness of R&D activity on the material welfare is again emphasized. Moreover, it holds both with and without public expenditure.

Finally, as shown in Figure CODPE 3.16, the amount of infrastructure at the end of the horizon is consistent and much greater than the quantity in all the preceding simulations in this chapter.

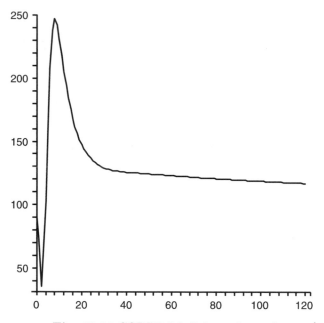

Fig. 12.23 CODPE 3.5: Labour demand

---

[6] Of course, the plausibility of these results depends, once more, on the temporal length of the single time period: one month, one trimester, one year, ...

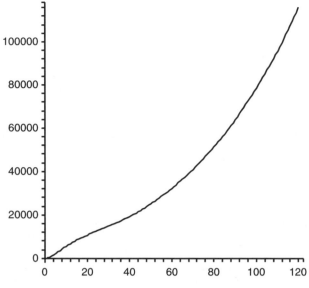

Fig. 12.24 CODPE 3.6: GDP

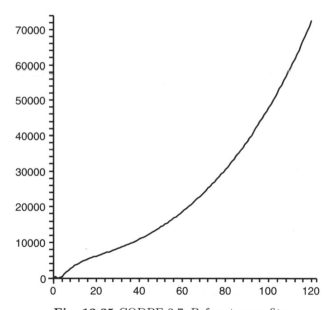

Fig. 12.25 CODPE 3.7: Before tax profits

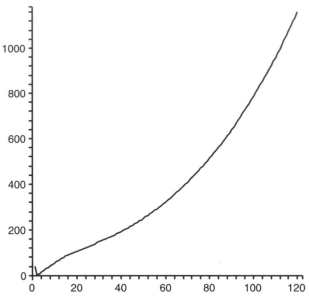

Fig. 12.26 CODPE 3.8: Pro capite product

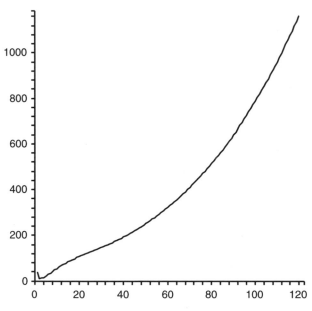

Fig. 12.27 CODPE 3.9: Production per worker

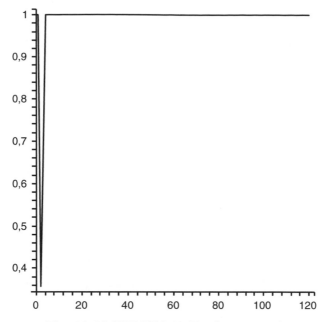

Fig. 12.28 CODPE 3.10: Employment ratio

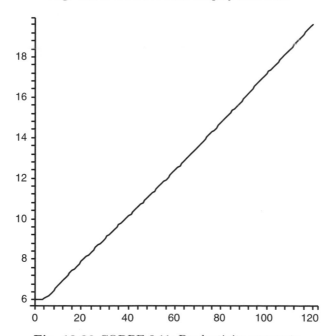

Fig. 12.29 CODPE 3.11: Productivity parameter

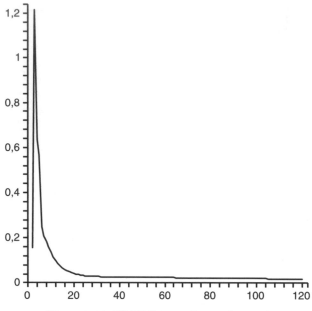

Fig. 12.30 CODPE 3.12: Rate of growth

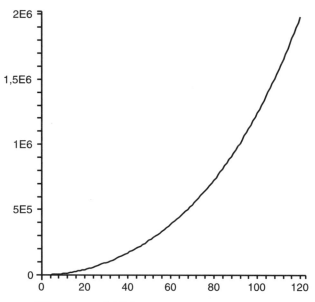

Fig. 12.31 CODPE 3.14: Total consumption

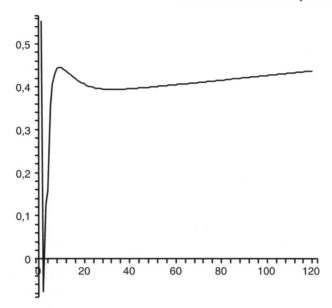

Fig. 12.32 CODPE 3.15: Percentage of after tax profits on GDP

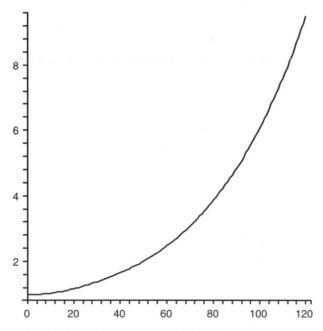

Fig. 12.33 CODPE 3.16: Infrastructure

12.3.2 Fourth CODPE-Simulation

Keeping the same parameter values for R&D and public expenditure as in the previous simulation, the other parameter values are the same as in the second simulation in Chapter 7, where there were cycles along the entire time horizon. For clarity, all these parameter values are repeated below:

$$\alpha = 0.2, \quad \beta = 0.5, \quad \delta = 0.2, \quad \epsilon = 0.01, \quad c = 0.1, \quad d = 0.5,$$

$$\tau = 0.3, \quad \kappa = 0.00001, \quad \eta = 0.1,$$

to which are added the starting values:

$$K_0 = 250, \quad w_0 = 5, \quad \theta_0 = 2, \quad Z_0 = 1,$$

which are the same values as in the second of the simulations presented in Chapter 7.

Note that the starting value of the productivity parameter is actually given by $\theta_0 = 2$, instead of the value 6 chosen in the three preceding simulations. This low value for θ explains the low value of total consumption obtained in this experiment, compared to the corresponding value in the third simulation.

Firstly, we can see that where oscillations occur, they are quite irregular and occur only in the first part of the time horizon. Once again, as in previous chapters, it is clear that, ceteris paribus, business cycles are very detrimental to the material welfare of individuals, despite the fact that these irregular cycles occur only in the first half of the chosen time horizon. Indeed, from Figure CODPE 4.14 it can be seen that total consumption takes the value $CT_{120} = 300000$, which is relatively poor compared to the value generated by the third simulation, $CT_{120} \approx 2 \times 10^6$.[7] One possible explanation is the efficiency values obtained by implementing this simulation, i.e. the total productivity parameter at the end of the time horizon, θ_{120}, and the corresponding amount of infrastructure, Z_{120}. These values, respectively, from Figure CODPE 4.11 and 4.16, $\theta_{120} = 11$ and $Z_{120} = 2$, should be compared to the corresponding values from the third simulation, i.e. $\theta_{120} = 19$ and $Z_{120} = 9$, where there are no cycles.

From Figures CODPE 4.1–2 we see that up to period 60 both total capital and wage rate take very low values, compared to the sustained growth from then on.

From Figures CODPE 4.4–5, it can be seen that, in the first half of the time horizon, both labour supply and labour demand are subject to irregular cycles: while GDP, which takes very low values up to period 40, follows qualitatively the same time path as total capital and wage rate, as shown in Figure CODPE4.6.

---

[7] But if we choose $\theta_0 = 6$, as in the preceding experiments, then the final value of total consumption is $CT_{120} \approx 1.8 \times 10^6$, which is comparable to, although less than, the corresponding value extracted from the third simulation.

Before tax profit shows the same time behaviour as capital and wage rate, as does per capita production, which however oscillates slightly between periods 16 and 20.

Production per worker is relatively low up to period 60, when it takes the value 18 after experiencing some slight oscillations; then explodes to reach 220 at the end of the horizon, as depicted in Figure CODPE4.9.

Employment ratio oscillates markedly between periods 20 and 28, and then equals 1; thereafter, full employment is constantly maintained.

Growth rate follows a slightly unusual time path, which is depicted in Figure CODPE4.12: after very marked oscillation between periods 12 and 20, it is subject to a number of very short, slight, and trend increasing oscillations up to period 60; thereafter it decreases smoothly to the end of the time horizon.

Percentage of after tax profits follows a similar time path, depicted in Figure CODPE4.15. In some senses, it shows a time behaviour that is also peculiar to the rate of growth: e.g., the percentage of after tax profits is subject to very gradual and trend decreasing short oscillations between periods 20 and 60; the rate of growth shows similar behaviour in the same time interval, but with an increasing trend.

Consumption behaves like capital and wage rate, while total consumption over time, as stated previously, takes a very limited value, i.e. $CT_{120} \approx 300000$:

Due to the small starting value of θ, and the existence of oscillations in the state variables, the final value for infrastructure endowment, as already noted, is only twice the starting value:

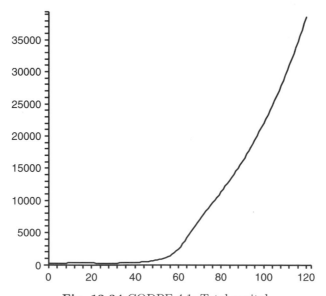

Fig. 12.34 CODPE 4.1: Total capital

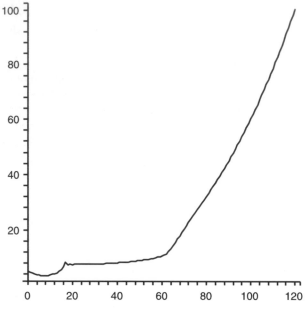

Fig. 12.35 CODPE 4.2: Wage rate

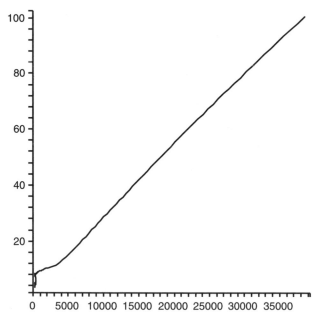

Fig. 12.36 CODPE 4.3: (K, w)-phase space

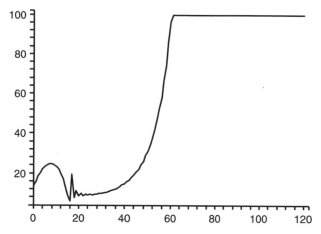

Fig. 12.37 CODPE 4.4: Labour supply

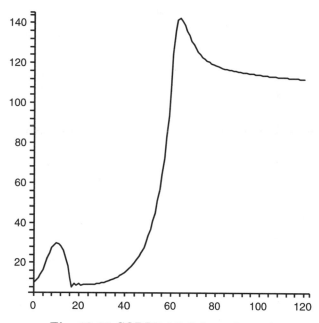

Fig. 12.38 CODPE 4.5: Labour demand

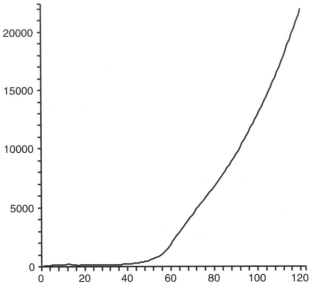

Fig. 12.39 CODPE 4.6: GDP

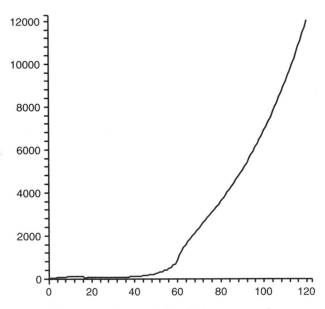

Fig. 12.40 CODPE 4.7: Before tax profits

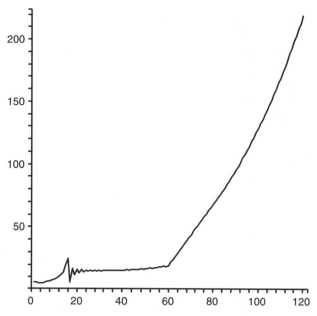

Fig. 12.41 CODPE 4.8: Pro capite product

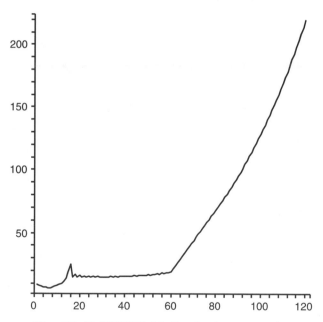

Fig. 12.42 CODPE 4.9: Production per worker

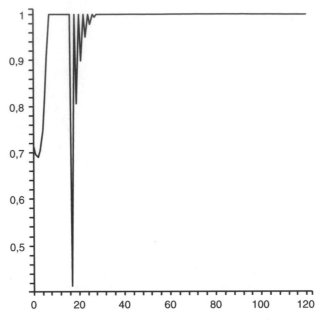

Fig. 12.43 CODPE 4.10: Employment ratio

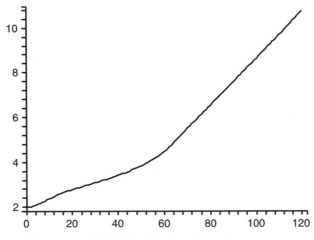

Fig. 12.44 CODPE 4.11: Productivity parameter

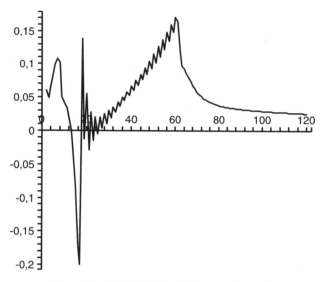

Fig. 12.45 CODPE 4.12: Rate of growth

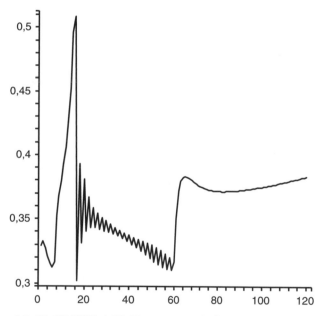

Fig. 12.46 CODPE 4.15: Percentage of after tax profits on GDP

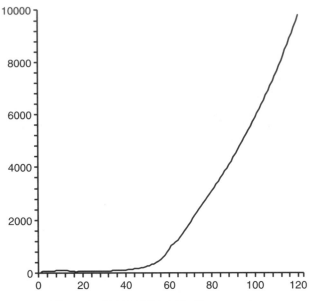

Fig. 12.47 CODPE 4.13: Consumption

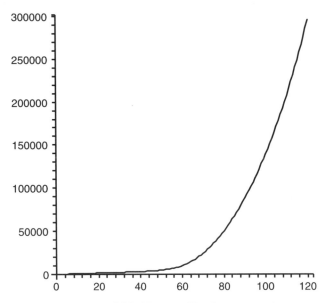

Fig. 12.48 CODPE 4.14: Total consumption

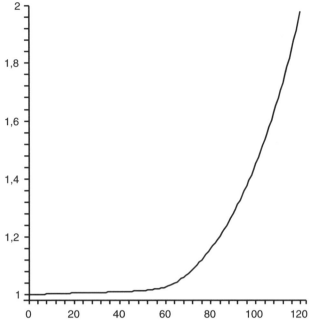

Fig. 12.49 CODPE 4.16: Infrastructure

12.3.3 Fifth CODPE-Simulation

With respect to the fourth simulation, the only parameter that changes is total productivity, which becomes $\theta_0 = 6$. All the time series that were subjected to cycles in the previous simulation present less extreme oscillations. We limit the presentation to those variables whose cycles were the most relevant in the fourth simulation, i.e. the rate of growth and percentage of after tax profit.

For comparison purposes, we also add the time path of total consumption, which proves that increasing the value of θ_0 has a very strong impact on the material welfare, compared with the fourth simulation.

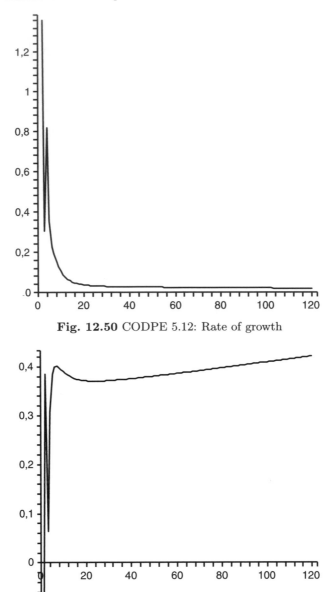

Fig. 12.50 CODPE 5.12: Rate of growth

Fig. 12.51 CODPE 5.15: Percentage of after tax profits on GDP

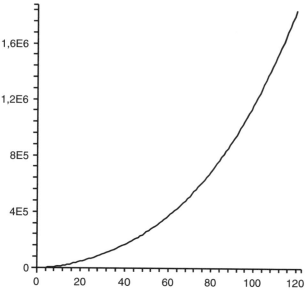

Fig. 12.52 CODPE 5.14: Total consumption

12.4 Conclusion

The main lesson from the simulations in this chapter, corroborated by those
in the preceding chapters, is that fluctuations have a negative impact on an
economy, with or without R&D and public expenditure.

It is sometimes argued that in recession phases inefficient production units
are closed down, thereby increasing the efficiency of the productive sector. This
is accompanied by a powerful stimulus to innovate by the surviving production units, to increase their efficiency in order to overcome the recession. But
the benefits derived from the so called "creative destruction" of Schumpeter-
ian memory, which is enhanced during recession periods, do not seem to be
confirmed by numerically implementing simple dynamic macromodels, such
as the ones presented here.

13

Material Welfare Comparisons

13.1 Motivation

To summarize, we report the final results of the simulations, expressed by material welfare obtained by the set of consumers–workers. This measure is identified with total undiscounted consumption, CT_{120}, enjoyed by all persons along the time horizon, $n = 120$. As we mentioned in the preface, considering no discount implies that all generations are treated on a par, as Ramsey long ago advocated.

Before turning to actual numbers, we should remember that when considering dynamic models on a bounded time horizon, scholars usually are faced with the problem of what happens to the economy after the last period. Indeed, strictly speaking, if consumption is the ultimate purpose of the economy then all capital ought to be literally "eaten up" in the last period, in order to maximize total consumption. But every real world economy continues to survive well beyond every chosen horizon; thus, some appropriate amount of capital must be transmitted to future generations, along with the existing production techniques.[1] In the models in this monograph, nothing else is required to put the economy into motion after the last considered period, since population and labour supply are considered as exogenous variables.

Moreover, the macroeconomic models presented and implemented in the chapters of this monograph solve, in a more natural way, the problem of the final endowment of capital. Indeed, we did not choose, as the objective of the economy, the maximization of total consumption, and zero final capital; rather we considered consumption in every period as determined by expending all labour income. This allowed us to consider, with reference also to the last time period, the same law governing the evolution of capital in all preceding

---

[1] In optimization models it is necessary either to introduce some specific end condition, e.g. the quantity of capital in existence at the end of the last period, as previously mentioned, or to let time increase with no bound. On this problem see, e.g., Dana et al. (2006).

time periods. Of course, this implies that final capital, K_{120}, is determined by the same mechanism as operated in all previous periods, thus supplying future generations with an appropriate quantity of capital.

13.2 Material Welfare Results

The following tables contain the values of total consumption, CT_{120}, generated by the simulations implemented in Chapters 7–12. Since in all cases of growing population, both for steady growth with final labour supply $L_{120} = 182$, and for logistic growth with final values $L_{120} = 120$, the labour force has a starting value $L_0 = 100$, total consumption is multiplied by the value $100/141$ for steady growing population simulations and by $100/110$ for logistic growing population simulations. The denominators, which are the mean values of corresponding populations,[2] allow us to obtain values of CT_{120} which are comparable to those in the case of no growth, where final populations always equal 100.

As a caveat to the above, we should repeat explicitly that the results presented for one set of simulations cannot be compared with the results obtained for another set, because parameters are frequently applied to different production functions and, moreover, are chosen with no reference to any specific real economy. What can be stated firmly, with reference to simulations differing from one another only in terms of the adjustment velocity parameter, α, is that ceteris paribus cycles do not promote material welfare.

Again, it should be remembered that total consumption is only an indicator of material welfare and, according to many scholars, perhaps only a very partial one. To promote happiness, in every modern society the so called **basic needs**, health, freedom, life expectancy at birth, education, housing, food, leisure, environment, ... are more important indicators than mere material welfare. But, in many respects, material welfare is positively and strongly correlated to all of these indicators; thus economics has a large say in promoting good living standards.

---

[2] I.e. an estimate of the average differences between the starting and the final values.

Table 13.1. Total Consumption for Stationary Labour Supply

Zero R&D activity

First COD Simulation: $CT_{120} \approx 492000$
Second COD Simulation: $CT_{120} = 6960$
Third COD Simulation: $CT_{120} \approx 14000$

Positive R&D Expenditure

Fourth COD Simulation: $CT_{120} \approx 543000$
Fifth COD Simulation: $CT_{120} \approx 1.84 \times 10^6$

Positive R&D and Public Expenditure

First CODPE Simulation: $CT_{120} \approx 380000$
Second CODPE Simulation: $CT_{120} \approx 400000$
Third CODPE Simulation: $CT_{120} \approx 2 \times 10^6$
Fourth CODPE Simulation: $CT_{120} \approx 300000$
Fifth CODPE Simulation: $CT_{120} \approx 1.8 \times 10^6$

Zero R&D expenditure

First CES Simulation: $CT_{120} \approx 5430$
Second CES Simulation: $CT_{120} \approx 167600$
Third CES Simulation: $CT_{120} = 352$
Fourth CES Simulation: $CT_{120} = 7850$

Positive R&D expenditure

Fifth CES Simulation: $CT_{120} = 208000$
Sixth CES Simulation: $CT_{120} = 6840$

Zero R&D expenditure

First LEO Simulation: $CT_{120} \approx 150000$
Second LEO b Simulation: $CT_{120} \approx 116000$

Positive R&D Expenditure

Fourth LEO Simulation: $CT_{48} \approx 64000$
Fifth LEO Simulation: $CT_{120} \approx 440000$

Table 13.2. Total Consumption for Steady Growing Labour Supply

Zero R&D Expenditure

First COD Simulation: $CT_{120} = 6965$

Positive R&D Expenditure

Second COD Simulation: $CT_{120} \approx 0.96 \times 10^6$
Third COD Simulation: $CT_{120} \approx 540000$

Table 13.3. Total Consumption for Logistic Growing Labour Supply

Zero R&D Expenditure

First COD Simulation: $CT_{120} \approx 6960$
Second COD Simulation: $CT_{120} \approx 57600$

Positive R&D Expenditure

Third COD Simulation: $CT_{120} \approx 2.5 \times 10^6$
Fourth COD Simulation: $CT_{120} \approx 3.8 \times 10^6$

Appendix: Representative Agent

1. Introduction

In spite of the fact that in the main text we consistently consider macroeconomic variables as the basic elements of the models presented here, we need to elaborate on the microeconomic foundations of macro variables, which help to explain the reversed S shaped form of the labour supply function. Indeed, no commodity can be produced if no labour input is available; but, of course, other (material) means of production are also needed to produce commodities.

Labour, considered as time spent to produce commodities, must be subtracted from time spent on leisure, given that for every individual the total time at his/her disposal in each time period is limited. Thus, it is quite natural to consider every family as equipped with a utility function that represents goods consumed in period t, C_t, and leisure time enjoyed at t, B_t.[3] Accordingly, considering the representative agent[4] as the unit of decision, each individual must choose how much to consume and how much to work in every period. Here we simply assume that the consumer acts in a very myopic way, and that he/she aims at maximizing his/her period t utility index, $u : \Re_+^2 \rightarrow \Re$, so that $u(C_t, B_t)$ is the current utility obtained by the agent when he/she consumes the pair (C_t, B_t).

2. Utility Maximization

In this monograph we have assumed that all consumers are workers, whose incomes are derived only from labour. According to the notations previously

---

[3] On family labour supply an interesting paper, both at the theoretical and at the applied level, is Blundell and Macurdy (1999).

[4] The usefulness of the representative agent is debated; e.g., Lippi (2005) is not in favour of introducing representative agents in macroeconomic models.

introduced, the income of all consumers in period t is $w_t L_t$,[5] which of course
in the considered macromodels means total labour income distributed among
the set of consumers–workers who are effectively employed. If $\bar{L}$, a positive
quantity, denotes total time disposability in every period, then, defining $B_t = \bar{L} - L_t$, since all consumers are identical at the macroeconomic level, the
problem is, given positive prices (p_t, w_t), to choose the non-negative pair,
(C_t, B_t), needed to maximize $u(C_t, B_t)$ under constraints

$$p_t C_t + w_t B_t = w_t \bar{L}, \tag{2.1}$$

$$L_t + B_t = \bar{L}. \tag{2.2}$$

In (2.1), which can be written $p_t C_t = w_t(\bar{L} - B_t)$, the price of leisure is w_t,
because every unit of leisure time is subtracted from labour time, whose unit
value is w_t.

Given the standard assumptions on u, i.e. that it is at least of class C^2,
has positive marginal utilities, $\partial u(C, B)/\partial C > 0$, $\partial u(C, B)/\partial B > 0$, and is
strictly quasi-concave, the preceding constrained maximum problem has one,
and only one, solution:

$$C_t = g_c(p_t, w_t), \tag{2.3}$$

$$B_t = g_b(p_t, w_t), \tag{2.4}$$

obtained by maximizing the Lagrangian

$$L_t(C_t, B_t, \lambda_t, \mu_t) = u(C_t, L_t) + \lambda_t(w_t \bar{L} - p_t C_t - w_t B_t) + \mu_t(\bar{L} - L_t - B_t),$$

where λ_t and μ_t are non-negative multipliers. The demand functions, g_c and
g_b, are continuous and positively homogeneous of zero degree, and they obvi-
ously satisfy the budget equality

$$p_t g_c(p_t, w_t) + w_t g_b(p_t, w_t) = w_t \bar{L} \tag{2.5}$$

for every positive pair (p_t, w_t).

3. Demand Functions for S Shaped Labour Supply

In the simulations presented in Part 3 the supply of labour, $L_t = \bar{L} - B_t$,
is assumed to have a reversed S shaped form; this implies that function g_b
has the corresponding particular shape. An interesting open problem is to
produce a utility function u capable of generating such a function g_b. The
theory of duality proves that under some, sufficient, conditions it is possible
to reconstruct a utility function given the corresponding demand functions.[6]

---

[5] Provided that $L_t = E_t$, i.e. that $L_t \leq N_t$, according to the notations introduced
in Chapter 2.

[6] On this problem, see Shephard (1970), Diewert (1982) and Scapparone (2005).

From a pragmatic point of view, we immediately know the demand function g_b corresponding to the labour supply function (2.1), introduced in Chapter 2 when population is stationary, since we can write

$$B_t = g_b(w_t, p_t) = \qquad\qquad (2.6)$$

$$= \bar{L} - \min\left\{\bar{L}, \max\{0, -a_0 + a_1 w_t/p_t - a_2(w_t/p_t)^2 + a_3(w_t/p_t)^3\}\right\}.$$

To simplify notations, let us define

$$\varXi(w/p) = -a_0 + a_1 w/p - a_2(w/p)^2 + a_3(w/p)^3.$$

From (2.6) we obtain:

$$B_t = 0 \text{ if } \min\left\{\bar{L}, \max\{0, \varXi(w_t/p_t)\}\right\} = \bar{L},$$
$$B_t = \bar{L} - \varXi(w_t/p_t) > 0 \text{ when } \min\left\{\bar{L}, \max\{0, \varXi(w_t/p_t)\}\right\} = \varXi(w_t/p_t),$$
$$B_t = \bar{L} \text{ if } \max\{0, \varXi(w_t/p_t)\} = 0.$$

Thus, from the budget constraint (2.5) we obtain

$$C_t = g_c(p_t, w_t) = (w_t/p_t)\bar{L} - (w_t/p_t)g_b(w_t, p_t), \qquad\qquad (2.7)$$

and there are three possibilities for g_c:

$$C_t = (w_t/p_t)\bar{L} \text{ if } \min\left\{\bar{L}, \max\{0, \varXi(w_t/p_t)\}\right\} = \bar{L},$$
$$C_t = \varXi(w_t/p_t)] \text{ for } \min\left\{\bar{L}, \max\{0, \varXi(w_t/p_t)\}\right\} = \varXi(w_t/p_t),$$
$$C_t = 0 \text{ when } \max\{0, \varXi(w_t/p_t)\} = 0.$$

The apparently unreasonable value of C_t in the last line, i.e. that consumption can equal zero in some cases, is a simple consequence of the assumption that at very low real wage rates, w_t/p_t, no labour is supplied, thus the corresponding income is zero, and consequently also consumption is zero. Of course, as all the computer simulations show, in equilibrium the real wage rate takes values at which labour supply is positive, and so consumption is also positive. If the reverse were true, the economy would be a starving one!

The point about these demand functions is that they cannot be inverted on their whole domain, because of their lack of monotonicity. Thus, it appears useless to try to find a utility function capable of generating the previous demand functions. It seems more fruitful to offer an explanation based on considering a population of consumers, grouped into families. In each family the members of working age vary from family to family, and families themselves differ from one another in their behaviour with respect to real income. Families choose to enter the labour market only when the real wage rate exceeds some minimum amount; moreover, among those families that do enter the labour market, some will choose to partly exit when the real wage rate is sufficiently high, maybe to re enter at extremely high real wage rates. It is obvious that this type of behaviour is dictated only in part by economic considerations: social and psychological considerations seem to play a large part.

4. Individual S Shaped Labour Supply Function

To elaborate a little more on the labour supply function, to obtain an individual labour supply with properties similar to those given in the main text for the global labour supply function, assume that a household has three target utilities: u_0 is the "reservation utility" level, which is independent of consumption and leisure, and is alternative to the utility obtained by the positive values for consumption and leisure; $\bar{u}$ denotes the "satisfaction utility" level (of course, we assume $\bar{u} > u_0$); moreover, the household has an "aspiration utility" level, u^*, satisfying $u^* > \bar{u}$, so that when the wage rate allows the household to obtain at least this utility, leisure time is reduced to zero and consumption takes the value $c = w\bar{\ell}$, where $\bar{\ell}$ means the total time disposability of the household.[7]

Let $u(c, b)$, an increasing function of c and b, denote the utility obtained by consuming c and enjoying leisure b; we can then put $u(0, \bar{\ell}) = u_0$. Choosing consumption as numeraire, $p_t = 1$, the household maximizes u under the budget constraint, $c + wb = w\bar{\ell}$. There are then four possibilities:

i) if solution (c, b) gives $u(c, b) \leq u_0$, then $b = \bar{\ell}$, and the household supplies zero labour time, thus $c = 0$;

ii) if $\bar{u} \geq u(c, b) > u_0$ then labour supply is $\bar{\ell} - b$, while consumption reaches $c = w(\bar{\ell} - b)$;

iii) if $u^* > u(c, b) > \bar{u}$ then when w increases leisure increases to b', and correspondingly consumption is $c' = w(\bar{\ell} - b')$, so to satisfy $u(c', b') = \bar{u} = u[w(\bar{\ell} - b'), b']$;

iv) if w reaches the value w^* verifying $u(c, b) = u[w^*(\bar{\ell} - b), b] = u^*$, then for all wage rates $w > w^*$ the household chooses $b = 0$ and $c = w\bar{\ell}$, because its aspiration level has been attained.

As an example, let $u(c, b) = \ln c + \rho \ln b$, where ρ is a positive parameter; by maximizing this function under the budget constraint, not considering u_0, $\bar{u}$, and u^*, we obtain:

$$c = \frac{1}{1+\rho} w\bar{\ell}, b = \frac{\rho}{1+\rho}\bar{\ell}, \quad u(c, b) = \ln\left(\frac{1}{1+\rho} w\bar{\ell}\right) + \rho \ln\left(\frac{\rho}{1+\rho}\bar{\ell}\right). \quad (2.8)$$

Thus, indirect utility is an increasing function of w. Moreover, assume that we have $\rho \ln\left(\frac{\rho}{1+\rho}\bar{\ell}\right) < u_0$, in order that case i) below can present itself at very low wage rates.

The four possibilities are:

i) if $u_0 \geq u(c, b)$ then we have $b = \bar{\ell}$: the household supplies no labour time and chooses $c = 0$;

---

[7] E.g., the aspiration utility level may express a sort of social utility so high that the household can consider itself as belonging to so called "high society".

ii) if $\bar{u} \geq u(c, b) > u_0$ then (c, b) has the value expressed by formulae (2.8), and labour supply jumps to $\bar{\ell} - b = \frac{1}{1+\rho}\bar{\ell}$, while of course consumption amounts to $c = \frac{1}{1+\rho}w\bar{\ell}$;

iii) if $u^* > u(c, b) > \bar{u}$ then the household chooses to increase leisure to b', and to consume $c' = w(\bar{\ell} - b')$, so that $u(c', b') = \bar{u}$, i.e. b' is chosen to satisfy $\ln[w(\bar{\ell} - b')] + \rho \ln b' = \bar{u}$, from which we derive $w = exp(\bar{u})/[(\bar{\ell} - b')b'^\rho]$, and thus

$$dw/db' = \frac{exp(\bar{u})b'^\rho}{[(\bar{\ell} - b')b'^\rho]^2}\left(1 + \rho - \rho\bar{\ell}/b'\right).$$

It can be seen that b' becomes an increasing function of w, and thus labour supply is a decreasing function of w, for $b' > \rho\bar{\ell}/(1 + \rho)$;

iv) when w reaches the value w^* verifying $\ln(w^*\bar{\ell}) = u^*$, i.e. when $w^* = exp(u^*)/\bar{\ell}$, then for every $w > w^*$ the household chooses $c = w\bar{\ell}$ and $b = 0$.

In summary, at very low wage rates consumption is an inferior commodity, while at very high wage rates leisure becomes an inferior commodity.

To obtain for the whole economy, a labour supply function of the type employed in the simulations we have to assume that there is a multitude of economically distinct households, all having the same utility function, but different values of ρ, and also possibly different values for $\bar{\ell}$, u_0, $\bar{u}$, and u^*. Then, at the aggregate level, the starting and ending jumps in individual labour supply are smoothed and at the limit, when there are numerous consumers, the labour supply function for the whole economy approximates that discussed in the main text.

References

1. Agarwal, R. P. (1992), *Difference Equations and Inequalities*, New York, Marcel Dekker.
2. Aghion, P., P. Howitt (1992), A Model of Growth Through Creative Destruction, *Econometrica*, 60, pp.323–351.
3. Aghion, P., P. Howitt (1998), *Endogenous Growth Theory*, Cambridge (MA), The MIT Press.
4. Allen, R. G. D. (1967), *Macro-Economic Theory*, London, Macmillan.
5. Amman, H. M., D. A. Kendrick, P. R. Mercado (2006), *Computational Economics*, Princeton (NJ), Princeton University Press.
6. Amman, H. M., D. A. Kendrick, J. Rust, eds. (1996), *Handbook of Computational Economics*, Amsterdam, North-Holland.
7. Arrow, K. J., H. B. Chenery, B. S. Minhas, R. M. Solow (1961), Capital-Labor Substitution and Economic Efficiency, *Review of Economics and Statistics*, 43, pp.225–250.
8. Ashenfelter, O. C., D. Card, eds. (1999), *Handbook of Labor Economics*, Amsterdam, North-Holland (3 vols.).
9. Ashenfelter, O. C., R. Layard, eds. (1986), *Handbook of Labor Economics*, Amsterdam, North-Holland (2 vols.).
10. Azariadis, C. (1993), *Intertemporal Macroeconomics*, Cambridge (MA), Blackwell.
11. Barro, R. J., X. Sala-i-Martin (2004), *Economic Growth*, Cambridge (MA), The MIT Press (second edition).
12. Blundell, R., T. Macurdy (1999), Labour Supply: a Review of Alternative Approaches, in O. C. Ashenfelter, D. Card, eds., cit., vol.3A, pp.1657–1672.
13. Dana, R., C. L. Van, T. Mitra and K. Nishimura, eds. (2006), *Handbook on Optimal Growth 1*, Berlin, Springer.
14. Diamond, P., ed. (1990), *Growth, Productivity, Unemployment*, Cambridge (MA), The MIT Press.
15. Diewert, W. E. (1982a), *Duality Theory in Economics*, Amsterdam, North-Holland.
16. Diewert, W. E. (1982b), Duality Approaches to Microeconomic Theory, *Handbook of Mathematical Economics* (K. J. Arrow and M. D. Intriligator, eds.), Amsterdam, North-Holland, vol.II, pp.535–599.

260   References

17. Gabisch, G., H.-W. Lorenz (1987), *Business Cycle Theory*, Berlin, Springer-Verlag.
18. Goodwin, R. M. (1967), A Growth Cycle, *Socialism, Capitalism and Economic Growth*, (C. H. Feinstein, ed.), Cambridge, Cambridge University Press, pp.54–58.
19. Grossman, G. M. and E. Helpman (1991), *Innovation and Growth in the Global Economy*, Cambridge (MA), The MIT Press.
20. Hicks, J. R. (1932), *The Theory of Wages*, London, Macmillan.
21. Hornung, D. (2002), *Investment, R&D, and Long-Run Growth*, Berlin, Springer.
22. Inada, K.-I. (1963), On a Two-Sector Model of Economic Growth, *The Review of Economic Studies*, 30(1), pp.119–127.
23. Kaldor, N. (1956), Alternative Theories of Distribution, *The Review of Economic Studies*, 23(2), pp.83–100.
24. Keynes, J. M. (1936), *The General Theory of Employment, Interest, and Money*, London, Macmillan.
25. Lippi, M. (2005), Aggregazione e microfondazioni della macroeconomia e della macroeconometria, *Eterogeneitá degli Agenti Economici e Interazione Sociale: Teorie e Verifiche Empiriche* (D. Delli Gatti and M. Gallegati, eds.), Bologna, il Mulino, pp.35–44.
26. Lucas, R. E. (1988), On the Mechanics of Economic Development, *Journal of Monetary Economics*, 22(1), pp. 3–42.
27. Matsuyama, K. (1999), Growing through Cycles, *Econometrica*, 67(2), pp. 335–347.
28. Miller, A. I. (2004), *Insights of Genius. Imagery and Creativity in Science and Art*, New York, Copernicus (Springer-Verlag).
29. Nicola, P. C. (2004), Macromodelli microfondati e mercato del lavoro, *Studi in onore di Mario Talamona* (G. Goisis, ed.), Padova, CEDAM, pp. 209–226.
30. Nicola, P. C. (2005), Micro-founded Macro-models and Labour Market, *Chaos, Solitons & Fractals*, 29, pp.671–680.
31. Nicola, P. C. (2007), Cycles and Growth in a Simple Macroeconomic Model (mimeo).
32. Pasinetti, L. L. (1962), Rate of Profit and Income Distribution in Relation to the Rate of Economic Growth, *The Review of Economic Studies*, 33(1), pp.267–279.
33. Phelps, E. S. (1968), Money-Wage Dynamics and Labour-Market Equilibrium, *Journal of Political Economy*, 76, pp.678–711.
34. Quadrio Curzio, A. (1971), *Investimenti in istruzione e sviluppo economico*, Bologna, il Mulino.
35. Ramsey, F. P. (1928), A Mathematical Theory of Saving, *The Economic Journal*, 38, pp.543–559.
36. Rivera–Batiz, L. A. and P. M. Romer (1991), Economic Integration and Endogenous Growth, *Quarterly Journal of Economics*, 106(2), pp. 531–555.
37. Romer, P. M. (1987), Growth Based on Increasing Returns Due to Specialization, *American Economic Review*, 77, pp.56–62.
38. Romer, P. M. (1990), Endogenous Technical Change, *Journal of Political Economy*, 98, pp.S71–S102.
39. Samuelson, P. A. (1970), *Economics*, New York, McGraw–Hill (eighth edition).
40. Scapparone, P. (2005), Costruzione di una funzione di utilitá tramite integrazione della funzione di domanda, *Economia Politica*, 22(2), pp.235–245.
41. Schumpeter, A. (1961), *The Theory of Economic Development*, New York, Oxford University Press, (translated from the German 1912 edition).

42. Shephard, R. W. (1970), *Theory of Cost and Production Functions*, Princeton (NJ), Princeton University Press.
43. Solow, R. M. (1956), A Contribution to the Theory of Economic Growth, *Quarterly Journal of Economics*, 70(1), pp.65–94.
44. Solow, R. M. (1990), *The Labor Market as a Social Institution*, Cambridge (MA), Blackwell.
45. Solow, R. M. (1998), *Work and Welfare*, Princeton (NJ), Princeton University Press.
46. Swan, T. W. (1956), Economic Growth and Capital Accumulation, *Economic Record*, 32, pp.334–361.
47. Uzawa, H. (1965), Optimum Technical Change in an Aggregative Model of Economic Growth, *International Economic Review*, 6(1), pp.18–31.
48. Walras, L. M. E. (1900), *Éléments d'économie politique pure*, Paris, Pichon et Durand-Auzias.
49. Wapler, R. (2003), *Unemployment, Market Structure and Growth*, Berlin, Springer.

Index

Lecture Notes in Economics and Mathematical Systems

For information about Vols. 1–519
please contact your bookseller or Springer-Verlag